CONSCIOUS LIVING

PROMISE KRÄMER

TABLE OF CONTENTS

INTRODUCTION

Reclaiming the Field

There is a moment in life when you begin to notice that something deeper is shaping your experience.

Not just circumstances.

Not just luck.

Not just other people.

Something internal.

You begin to sense that the way you interpret events, the way you hold stories, the way you react, the way you rehearse thoughts — all of it forms an atmosphere around you.

An internal world.

And that internal world seems to organize your external one more than you previously understood.

This book is about that world.

I call it the field.

I was born in Soweto. Raised there. Loved it there.

And like many who grow up in complex systems — where history, poverty, resilience, faith, trauma, hope, and rupture coexist — I was introduced early to powerful narratives about influence.

Witches.

Blessings.

Curses.

Destiny.

Helpers.

Intruders.

Favor.

Misfortune.

Some of those narratives protect communities.

Some create cohesion.

Some preserve wisdom.

And some create fear.

Over the years — through my own lived experience, through dreams, through ritual practice, through constellation work, through watching families fracture under accusation, through watching people rebuild after devastation — one truth kept surfacing:

The most powerful force shaping our lives is not intrusion.

It is participation.

Not what is done to us.

But how we organize internally around what happens.

That internal organizing space — the field — is what this book explores.

You already know the field.

You enter it when you are fully present in a conversation, and time disappears.

You enter it when grief quiets everything else.

You enter it when resentment replays a story for years.

You enter it when imagination builds a future before it physically exists.

You enter it when you spiral.

You enter it when you are clear.

The field is not mystical.

It is your conscious internal environment.

And it is creative.

This book is not a religious text.

It is not anti-religion either.

It is not dismissive of ancestral belief, spiritual archetypes, or ritual practice.

It is not here to mock culture.

It is here to deepen understanding.

To bring sovereignty back to the individual without stripping away the richness of inherited language.

We will speak about:

Influence.

Witchcraft narratives.

Addiction.

Justice.

Revenge.

Forgiveness.

Creation.

Time.

Rhythm.

Presence.

Embodiment.

Meaning.

But we will speak about them through one central lens:

What is happening in the field?

And how do we live responsibly inside it?

Conscious living is not about controlling outcomes.

It is about regulating participation.

It is about cleaning your field when it becomes crowded.

Naming emotions before they dominate.

Releasing what poisons.

Creating intentionally.

Allowing time.

Holding ethics.

Forgiving wisely.

Returning to presence.

It is practical.

It is daily.

It is deeply human.

If you are here because life has felt turbulent,

if you have wondered whether someone has influenced your path,

if you have felt stuck, behind, cursed, rushed, angry, overwhelmed,

if you have struggled with resentment, addiction, comparison, or fear

—

you are not alone.

But you are also not powerless.

This book is an invitation to reclaim authorship.

Not aggressively.

Not arrogantly.

But consciously.

The field is already active in your life.

The question is not whether it exists.

The question is:

Will you participate in it deliberately?

Let us begin.

Welcome

In this book, we are about to dive into inner worlds.

Not imaginary worlds. Not fantasy. Not escape.

But the actual inner world you inhabit every single day — the one that shapes your reactions, your relationships, your work, your creativity, your conflicts, your peace.

Most of us live inside this world unconsciously.

Sometimes we enter it deliberately — in dreams, in deep conversation, in prayer, in meditation, in ritual, in love, in grief, in creative flow. But more often, we are moved by it without realizing that we are inside it.

This book is about becoming conscious within that world.

It is about learning to access it intentionally, to relate within it responsibly, and to create from it deliberately.

Before we go further, we need shared language.

We need to define the key words that will guide this work.

The Structure of This Book

This book unfolds in five core movements:

1. The Field – understanding the inner world as an actual field of participation.
2. Relations – understanding how connection forms reality.
3. Doorways – learning how to access the field consciously.
4. Creation – understanding how we bring things into being through the field.
5. Processing – integrating daily life through conscious field access.

We will first establish understanding.

Then we will move into practice.

And finally, into integration — what I call conscious living.

Let us begin with the foundation.

1. The Field

In physics, a field is not a thing — it is a space of influence. A gravitational field, an electromagnetic field — invisible, yet structuring movement and interaction.

In psychology, people speak of the mind.

In spirituality, they speak of the spirit.

In constellations, we speak of the knowing field.

In religion, one might speak of the Word, or the breath that brings life.

Different languages. Same pointing.

The field, as we will use it here, is the inner world of living participation.

It is not merely your thoughts.

It is not just imagination.

It is not a metaphor.

It is an actual layer of lived experience — a relational environment that you enter, and that moves through you.

You enter the field when you are fully absorbed in a conversation and lose track of time.

You enter it when you are dreaming.

You enter it when you are "in the zone."

You enter it in ritual.

You enter it in grief.

You enter it in love.

In my own work in constellations, whenever I step into a representing role, I enter the field. Something larger than personal thought begins to move. But the same happens when I sit with a friend, and we are fully present with what is unfolding between us. There is a shared field. A relational atmosphere. A living exchange.

We inhabit this world constantly — but rarely consciously.

This book is not about escaping into the field.

It is about recognizing that you are already inside it.

2. Relations

If the field is the environment, relations are the architecture.

Nothing in existence stands alone.

Physics tells us that stable matter forms through relational bonds. Hydrogen and oxygen form water — not because either is water on its own, but because of how they relate. Atoms bind. Molecules stabilize. Structures emerge through relationships.

Creation is relational.

Without relation, there is no structure. Without structure, there is no stability. Without stability, there is no form.

This applies to matter.

It applies to ecosystems.

It applies to families.

It applies to identity.

You are not only an individual — you are a network of relations.

You are related to your parents.

To your children.

To your partner.

To your work.

To your body.

To your memories.

To your beliefs.

To your dreams.

And here is the deeper question:

Are these relations conscious?

Because relations form structure.

And structure forms life.

If water forms through the correct bonding of elements, then your life forms through the bonding of your relations.

This is where relational hygiene becomes essential.

Relational hygiene means asking:

What am I relating to?

How am I relating?

What patterns are forming through these bonds?

Are these relations creating stability — or tension?

Are they conscious — or reactive?

You cannot avoid relating.

But you can become conscious of what you are building through your relations.

3. Doorways to the Field

The field is always present.

The question is whether you have access.

Dreams are one doorway — whether sleeping dreams or waking imagery. In dreams, you enter the field without resistance. Lucidity simply means becoming aware while inside it.

Meditation is another doorway.

Prayer is another.

Ritual.

Ukuphahla — being deeply present, attentive, and available with ancestral knowledge

Flow states in creative work.

Moments of full relational presence.

The present moment itself is an access point.

But here is the caution:

If you are not consciously accessing the field, it still moves you.

Other people's emotions, inherited patterns, cultural narratives — these can shape your direction if you remain reactive. Without intentional awareness, the field can pull you rather than you participating within it.

Conscious access shifts you from being driven — to driving.

4. Creation

Everything creates.

We have heard this across generations.

Manifestation teachings.

Religious language about "the Word."

Scientific language about emergence.

Ideas become things.

But where do ideas merge?

Where do impulses organize before they become action?

In the field.

The field is where possibility gathers. Where relational bonds form before matter stabilizes. Where meaning precedes movement.

Understanding the field is crucial if you wish to create consciously.

Your career is a form of hunting — gathering resources for yourself and your children.

Your relationships cultivate emotional nourishment.

Your creative projects cultivate joy.

All of these are acts of creation.

When you remain in contact with the field, you remain in contact with your creative ground.

When you lose contact, you begin to react instead of create.

5. Processing

Finally — processing.

Processing means integrating experience correctly into your system.

Every day, you take in impressions. Conversations. Tensions. Joys. Conflicts. Micro-moments. Unfinished emotions.

If these are not processed, they accumulate.

Processing is not overthinking.

It is not an analysis.

It is allowing experience to reorganize within the field so it does not remain stuck in your body, your mind, or your relational patterns.

Processing is digestion.

Just as the body digests food, your field must digest experience.

This book will teach you how.

Where We Go From Here

We will first deepen your understanding of the field.

Then we will examine relations — because nothing stands alone.

Then we will explore the doorways — through exercises and practices.

And from there, we move into integration — into the lived application of conscious living.

You are not learning something foreign.

You are learning to become aware of where you already are.

Welcome.

PART ONE
DEFINING AND APPLYING FIELD ACCESS

There is a place you have been entering your whole life, often without knowing it.

I call it the field.

Not as a mystical escape. Not as philosophy for philosophy's sake. But as a framework for processing life — for digesting what happens to you, around you, and within you.

Conscious Living begins here.

The field is not somewhere else. It is not reserved for mystics, prophets, or those who meditate for hours. It is an accessible layer of awareness in which experience reorganizes itself correctly inside you. It is where stuck dynamics loosen. It is where confusion rearranges into clarity. It is where pain integrates without you having to force change in the outer world.

And this is important:

Processing does not require changing the situation.

You do not need to fix your partner. You do not need to control your child. You do not need to win the argument or solve the workplace tension. When an experience is integrated correctly into your internal system, it loses its charge. The outer may remain the same — but you are no longer entangled in it.

The core aim of this work is simple:

To cultivate awareness so you can access the field consciously.

Entry Pathways

You already know some of the doors.

Dreams are one. Whether sleeping or awake, you enter the field nightly. Lucid dreaming simply makes this entry conscious. Ritual, meditation, and prayer are others. Each of these practices quiets the surface mind and softens the body enough for perception to shift.

With practice, access becomes easier. What once required a silent forest or a long meditation may eventually happen in a parked car, a quiet kitchen, or while sitting on the edge of your bed.

Many people discover what I call portal places — locations where entry feels natural. Often, these are natural environments. Streams. Rivers. Oceans. A particular tree. A specific bench overlooking water. There is something about quiet observation in the presence of nature — especially water — that reorganizes our internal rhythm.

Water does not rush. It moves.

And so do you.

Preparing the Body and Environment

Before deliberately entering the field, attend to the basics.

Observe your surroundings. Are you safe? Do you have enough time? Are you rushing? The field does not respond well to urgency. If your nervous system is alert and scanning for danger, perception will remain contracted.

Drink water. Adjust your posture. Make sure your body is comfortable. Small cues signal safety to the system. When the body relaxes, awareness widens.

If something feels off — address it. A missing piece in the physical environment will keep pulling you back into surface consciousness. Adjust first. Enter second.

Recognizing Entry

How do you know you are in the field?

You may forget where you are or how you arrived at a particular internal scene. The usual mental commentary quiets. Thoughts slow down or dissolve.

Scenarios may begin to form without you selecting them. Images, sensations, or movements appear — almost dream-like — yet you remain aware.

Sometimes there is darkness. With eyes closed, you see "nothing," yet perception feels active. Even with eyes open, the environment may soften or fade to the background.

Do not force this.

Allow the field to lead.

Your only task is awareness.

Awareness is the anchor.

Anchoring and Scanning

When entering deliberately, it helps to begin with an anchor — a gentle question or area of attention.

Before diving into a specific issue, perform an overall scan. Notice your work life. Your romantic or marital dynamics. Your general well-being. Observe lightly. Do not fixate. If something stands out, you may jot it down later. But inside the field, you remain a witness first.

You may then choose a specific issue for deeper inquiry.

Framing the Inquiry

Only ask from stillness.

If your body is agitated or your mind is racing — wait. The inquiry must come from a calm, present state — beyond mental chatter, beyond physical discomfort. Fully here. Fully aware.

Craft the question simply. Short. Direct. No analysis.

Not:

"Why is my child acting like this, and what does this mean about our attachment and my parenting style?"

Instead:

"Why are we fighting so much?"

Then send the question into the field.

And return to stillness.

Do not chase an answer.

Observing the Response

The response may appear as scenery. A memory. A moment. A felt sense of conflict. Perhaps you see yourself and your child arguing. Perhaps you feel the tension before it even manifests outwardly.

Stay seated. Stay physically where you are.

You are watching the field — not re-entering the fight.

Curiosity replaces reactivity.

Each field speaks differently. For some, it is visual. For others, sensory. For others, relational — a knowing without image. There is no correct format. There is only your practice.

Bringing the Field Into Daily Life

Eventually, this is no longer something you "do."

You begin to observe field movements in real time.

During a conversation, you feel the shift before words escalate. In a meeting, you sense the unspoken dynamic. At home, you recognize when you are about to repeat a pattern.

You step slightly outside the identification.

You witness your field in motion.

This is relational awareness — tracking how you move toward others, how they move toward you, and how patterns form between you.

The goal is not escape. It is integration.

Field access returns you to daily life with greater clarity, less entanglement, and a deeper sense of responsibility for how you participate in reality.

This is conscious living.

PART TWO
RELATIONS

If the field is the environment we inhabit, then relations are the forces that shape what forms within it.

Nothing exists in isolation.

Not in physics.

Not in biology.

Not in families.

Not in identity.

A single hydrogen atom is not water. A single oxygen atom is not water. Yet when they bond in a specific relational structure, something entirely new stabilizes. Water emerges — with properties neither element holds alone.

Matter forms through relation.

Creation stabilizes through relation.

Life organizes through relation.

This is not poetry. It is structure.

Atoms bind. Cells coordinate. Ecosystems balance themselves through intricate networks of mutual dependence. Even the body you call "mine" is a collaboration — organs communicating, systems responding, signals traveling, relationships regulating.

Without relation, there is no structure.

Without structure, there is no stability.

Without stability, there is no lived form.

Now bring this closer.

You are not a single, sealed individual.

You are a web of relations.

You are related to your parents — whether you speak to them or not.

To your children — whether they are near you or grown.

To your partner, your colleagues, your ancestors, your teachers.

To your body.

To your history.

To your future.

To your work.

To your dreams.

Each of these relations forms a structure inside your field.

And structure shapes how your life stabilizes.

This is why relational awareness is not optional. It is foundational.

What Is a Relation?

A relation is not merely a connection.

It is an active exchange of influence.

In physics, particles influence one another through fields. In biology, organisms co-regulate through feedback loops. In psychology, attachment shapes perception. In systemic work, patterns repeat across generations because relations transmit more than words ever do.

A relation is an influence.

A relation is an exchange.

A relation is participation.

You are constantly participating in relational systems — even when you think you are acting alone.

The way you respond to criticism.

The way you withdraw in conflict.

The way you over-function, under-function, rescue, avoid, dominate, and submit.

These are relational patterns.

And patterns form structures.

Relational Hygiene

If relations build structure, then we must speak about hygiene.

Relational hygiene is not about cutting people off.

It is not about moral judgment.

It is about awareness.

What am I relating to?

How am I relating?

Is this relation reactive or conscious?

What does this bond produce in my life?

Just as certain atomic bonds create stability and others create volatility, certain relational patterns stabilize your inner system — and others destabilize it.

Some relations generate clarity.

Some generate confusion.

Some generate vitality.

Some generate depletion.

Relational hygiene means observing the bonds you form — both internally and externally.

Are you bonded to resentment?

To old narratives?

To inherited loyalties that no longer serve your current life?

To expectations that create tension instead of alignment?

Or are you consciously bonding to creativity?

To responsibility?

To clarity?

To the truth?

You cannot stop relating.

But you can become conscious of what your relations are creating.

Creation Is Relational

Creation never happens in isolation.

Even the mythic idea of "the Word" bringing life into being speaks to relation — vibration meeting substance. Sound meeting form. Influence meeting receptivity.

Manifestation teachings point toward the same truth: what you hold in relation, you shape.

But this is not about magical thinking.

It is about structure.

When you repeatedly relate to fear, your life organizes around defense.

When you repeatedly relate to opportunity, your life organizes around expansion.

When you repeatedly relate to resentment, your relational bonds tighten around conflict.

Your life stabilizes according to the relations you sustain.

Just as water forms from specific bonding patterns, your lived reality forms from the patterns you continuously reinforce.

The Responsibility of Relation

This is where the book becomes practical.

You are not merely reacting to life.

You are participating in forming it.

Every relation strengthens a structure in your field.

Every repeated pattern deepens a bond.

Every conscious shift alters the architecture.

Relational awareness allows you to see:

What am I building?

Not in theory.

But in daily life.

Because conscious living begins with recognizing that nothing you relate to is neutral.

Relation creates form.

And form becomes life.

Relations in Daily Life

It is easy to speak about atoms bonding and ecosystems stabilizing. It becomes uncomfortable when we realize that the same laws operate in our kitchen, our marriage, our inbox, and our nervous system.

Let me give you examples.

Example 1: The Morning Tone

You wake up.

Your partner says something sharp.

You have options — but you don't experience them as options. You experience them as a reflex.

You tighten.

You defend.

You withdraw.

Or you over-explain.

Now pause.

What just happened?

A relational bond is activated.

Perhaps you are bonded to the pattern: I must defend myself to stay safe.

Or: I must keep the peace at all costs.

Or: I disappear when tension rises.

The moment itself is small. But the underlying relation is structured.

If you repeatedly respond in the same way, you are reinforcing a bond. And that bond stabilizes into identity.

"I am the one who always has to fix things."

"I am the one who gets blamed."

"I am the calm one."

"I am the explosive one."

But these are not personalities.

They are relational stabilizations.

Example 2: The Child Who "Triggers" You

Your child refuses to listen. Again.

You feel heat rising.

But what are you relating to?

Are you relating to the child in front of you?

Or to the part of you that once felt unheard?

Or to an inherited belief about authority?

Or to fear that you are failing?

Very often, we are not relating to the present moment.

We are relating to accumulated, unprocessed structures inside our field.

Relational hygiene here would mean pausing long enough to ask:

What am I actually bonded to in this moment?

Because if you are bonded to your own fear of inadequacy, your reaction will reinforce that structure. If you shift your bond — to curiosity, to firmness without fear, to presence — the entire relational field changes.

Same child.

Different bond.

Different outcome.

Example 3: Work and Identity

You receive feedback at work.

Immediately, your stomach drops.

Why?

Because you are not just relating to the feedback.

You are relating to worth.

You are bonded to the idea that performance equals value.

Now the entire field tightens.

Instead of seeing feedback as information, you experience it as a threat.

Relational hygiene in this case might mean consciously shifting your bond:

"I relate to growth — not to perfection."

"I relate to feedback as refinement — not as rejection."

That shift changes how your nervous system organizes the experience.

And that changes your life trajectory.

Micro-Relations

Here is something subtle.

Not all relations are dramatic.

You are constantly relating in micro-moments.

- How you speak to yourself after making a mistake.
- How you relate to your body when you look in the mirror.
- How you relate to money — as scarcity, as a tool, as a burden, as an opportunity.
- How you relate to rest — as laziness or as nourishment.

Each of these relations forms an internal structure.

If every time you are tired, you relate to yourself with criticism, you are bonding fatigue to shame.

If every time you succeed, you minimize it, you are bonding achievement to unworthiness.

If every time you feel joy, you expect loss, you are bonding happiness to anxiety.

These bonds accumulate.

And accumulation becomes reality.

Inherited Relations

Now we go one layer deeper.

Many of your strongest relational bonds were not consciously chosen.

They were modeled.

Inherited.

Absorbed.

Perhaps in your family:

- Conflict meant silence.
- Success meant threat.
- Emotion meant weakness.
- Love meant sacrifice.

Without realizing it, you bond to these patterns.

You enter adulthood thinking:

"This is just who I am."

But what if it is simply what you learned to relate to?

When you begin to observe your relations, you begin to see that identity is not fixed — it is structured.

And what is structured can be restructured.

Conscious Re-Bonding

This is where practice begins.

Relational hygiene is not about cutting everything off.

It is about re-bonding intentionally.

Instead of bonding to resentment, you bond to clarity.

Instead of bonding to fear, you bond to responsibility.

Instead of bonding to chaos, you bond to rhythm.

Instead of bonding to reactivity, you bond to awareness.

This does not happen through force.

It happens through repeated, conscious participation.

Every time you pause instead of react — you loosen an old bond.

Every time you respond from presence — you strengthen a new one.

Every time you process instead of suppress — you reorganize structure.

And slowly, your field stabilizes differently.

The Practical Question

So, here is the daily question:

What am I bonding with right now?

Not philosophically.

Right now.

In this conversation.

In this tension.

In this joy.

In this decision.

Because relation creates structure.

Structure creates experience.

Experience becomes life.

You are building something every day.

The only question is whether you are building it consciously.

And this is why relations matter.

PART THREE
THE DOORWAY -
AND THE QUIET WORK OF CREATION

I want to slow this down.

Because the doorway is not something you storm through.

It is something you notice.

It is something you remember.

For me, the doorway began long before I had language for it.

It began with a dream.

The First Door

When I was a little girl, my mother fetched us from my paternal grandparents, where we had been living. Shortly after that, my grandfather passed away — but she did not tell me immediately.

One night, I dreamt of him.

He was calling me.

Not in a frightening way. Not in a dramatic way. Just calling me, using my childhood name. In the dream, it felt natural. Familiar. As though I could go to him.

I woke up excited.

"I saw Mukuru. I saw Grandpa. He was calling me."

My mother's face changed. She became frightened. Very clear. Very firm.

"The next time you see him in your dream, and he calls you, don't go to him. He has passed away."

Something shifted in me that day.

As a child, I internalized something very quietly:

I have a choice in my dream.

I can go.

Or I can not go.

That was the first doorway.

I did not have the word "lucid." I did not know about field access. But I understood something — there was a layer of reality I could enter consciously.

The Second Door

In our home, dreams were not ignored.

Every morning, before we were allowed to speak of anything else, we had to recall what we had dreamed. My father would ask us. Sometimes he would take our dreams as signals for his own life.

As a child, it was exhausting. Annoying. I just wanted to talk. But instead, I had to remember.

And then there was another rule — one common in many Southern African belief systems: you should not eat in your dreams.

No one explained why. But it was serious.

So, one night, in a dream, I was about to eat. And something in me paused.

How did I get here?

Am I dreaming?

And suddenly — I was aware.

I didn't eat.

I moved through the dream knowing I was in a dream.

That became a trigger.

Whenever I was about to eat in a dream, I would check.

Whenever something felt slightly off, I would check.

Am I awake?

Or am I dreaming?

My father never took those dreams seriously. He dismissed them. "You watch too much TV." But to me, they were real in a different way.

They were the beginning of consciously living inside the field.

A Teenage Life Between Worlds

From around twelve until I left home at eighteen, I lucid-dreamed almost daily.

I looked forward to sleeping.

I missed teenage parties. I missed a lot of things. I was always sleeping.

But I was not escaping.

I was building.

My parents were mostly not home. My father was a taxi driver, often at the rank. My mother worked at the hospital, sometimes staying away for a week at a time. I was the adult in the house.

So I slept.

And in that sleeping life, I created.

It wasn't random chaos. It was structured. I built a life there — relationships, environments, experiences.

Strangely, that life resembles my life now.

Not in exact detail. But in feeling.

The tone.

The harmony.

The sense of belonging.

The laughter of children near water.

I remember once sitting by a lake with my children. I was reading. They were laughing loudly, freely. And something in my body paused.

Have we been here before?

I searched my memory.

Then I knew.

It was not déjà vu.

It was a lucid dream.

Years before.

The axis of that dream — and many like it — was care.

Care was the center. Everything revolved around it.

The Field as Training Ground

Some may look at that childhood and say:

That was loneliness.

That was absence.

That was too much responsibility.

And yes — perhaps.

But it was also training.

Because lucid dreaming did not end when I woke up.

I carried the question into the day:

Am I awake?

I became observant. Quiet. Alert.

Not just spiritually alert — but also physically alert. We lived in a relatively unsafe area. I was often alone. I had to sense danger before it arrived.

So, I learned to feel the field.

Where am I in relation to these people?

What is moving underneath what is being said?

Where is tension gathering?

How do I maneuver?

I did not call it field awareness.

But that is what it was.

The doorway was not only in sleep. It was in the presence.

Doorway and Creation

This is why I say the doorway and creation are inseparable.

When you enter the field consciously, you are not just observing.

You are participating.

In my lucid dreams, I was not just watching scenes. I was choosing. I was deciding not to go with my grandfather. I was choosing not to eat. I was exploring environments with awareness.

That practice strengthened something.

It strengthened the muscle of intentional participation.

Later in life, when my outer world slowed down — when my environment became more stable, more balanced — I could bring that same awareness into daily life.

Now, instead of asking, "Am I dreaming?"

I ask, "What is the axis right now?"

Fear?

Control?

Care?

And when I shift the axis, life reorganizes.

Creation Is Quiet

Creation is not a loud manifestation.

It is not shouting desires into the universe.

It is subtle.

It is choosing the center from which you move.

As a teenager, I did not know I was rehearsing my future. But I was stabilizing a feeling — a field tone — of care, safety, laughter, water, belonging.

Years later, I find myself inside it.

This does not mean dreams are predictions.

It means the field organizes around repeated relational centers.

If you repeatedly live inside fear, fear becomes structure.

If you repeatedly live inside care, care becomes structure.

The doorway gives you access to that layer.

The Invitation

Your doorway may not be lucid dreaming.

It may be:

- The moment before you respond in conflict.
- The silence after prayer.
- The softness that comes in meditation.
- The stillness in nature.
- The instant you feel yourself about to react — and instead you pause.

That pause is the door.

And on the other side of it is creation.

Not fantasy.

Structure.

You are already inside the field.

The question is not whether you can enter.

The question is:

From what axis are you creating?

PART FOUR
PROCESSING - RITUAL, DIGESTION, AND LETTING THINGS FIND THEIR PLACE

Let's bring this closer.

Processing is digestion.

Not mentally replaying.

Not fixing.

Not forcing forgiveness.

Digestion means allowing what entered your space to move — and to find its rightful place within your field.

As a conscious being, I must process what I allow into my space.

Conversations.

Conflicts.

Big ruptures.

Disappointments.

Decisions.

If they remain undigested, they stay suspended in the field. And what is suspended begins to shape you quietly.

For smaller things, a pause is enough.

For bigger stories — ruptures, deep relational patterns, long-standing tensions — ritual becomes important.

Ritual creates a container.

And container allows movement.

Why Ritual Matters

We often think of ritual as religious, dramatic, or cultural.

But ritual is simply an intentional structure.

It is saying:

"This matters.

I am entering this consciously."

When you mark space, light a candle, or designate a time, you are signaling to your nervous system and to your field:

We are working now.

That shift alone deepens processing.

Because the field responds to intention.

A Simple Mini-Consolation Ritual

I want to give you something practical.

This is a practice I began years ago. I did not have language for it then. It was simply what my system needed.

It helped me with my relationship with my mother. It helped me with work decisions. It helped me reorganize internal patterns that felt stuck.

You will need:

- A few A4 papers
- A pen
- A quiet space
- Optional: a candle, soft light, or gentle sound

First, take care of the physical.

Make sure you have time.

Make sure you will not be interrupted.

Make sure your children are cared for, your phone is off, and your body is not hungry or rushed.

Physical safety allows emotional movement.

Step 1: Name the Elements

On each paper, write one word.

Only one word.

For example:

"Mother"

"Work"

"Money"

"Our Conflict"

"Partner"

"Children"

Do not write stories. Do not explain. One word holds the essence.

Place the papers on the floor in different positions.

Do not overthink placement.

Let it be intuitive.

Step 2: Mark the Space

Light your candle if you wish.

Quietly say to yourself:

"I am entering this to process, not to fix."

That sentence is important.

Processing is not control.

It is digestion.

Step 3: Slow Movement

Begin standing on one paper.

Do not analyze.

Just stand.

Notice:

How does your body feel here?

Is there tension?

Pull?

Resistance?

Softness?

Then slowly move to another paper.

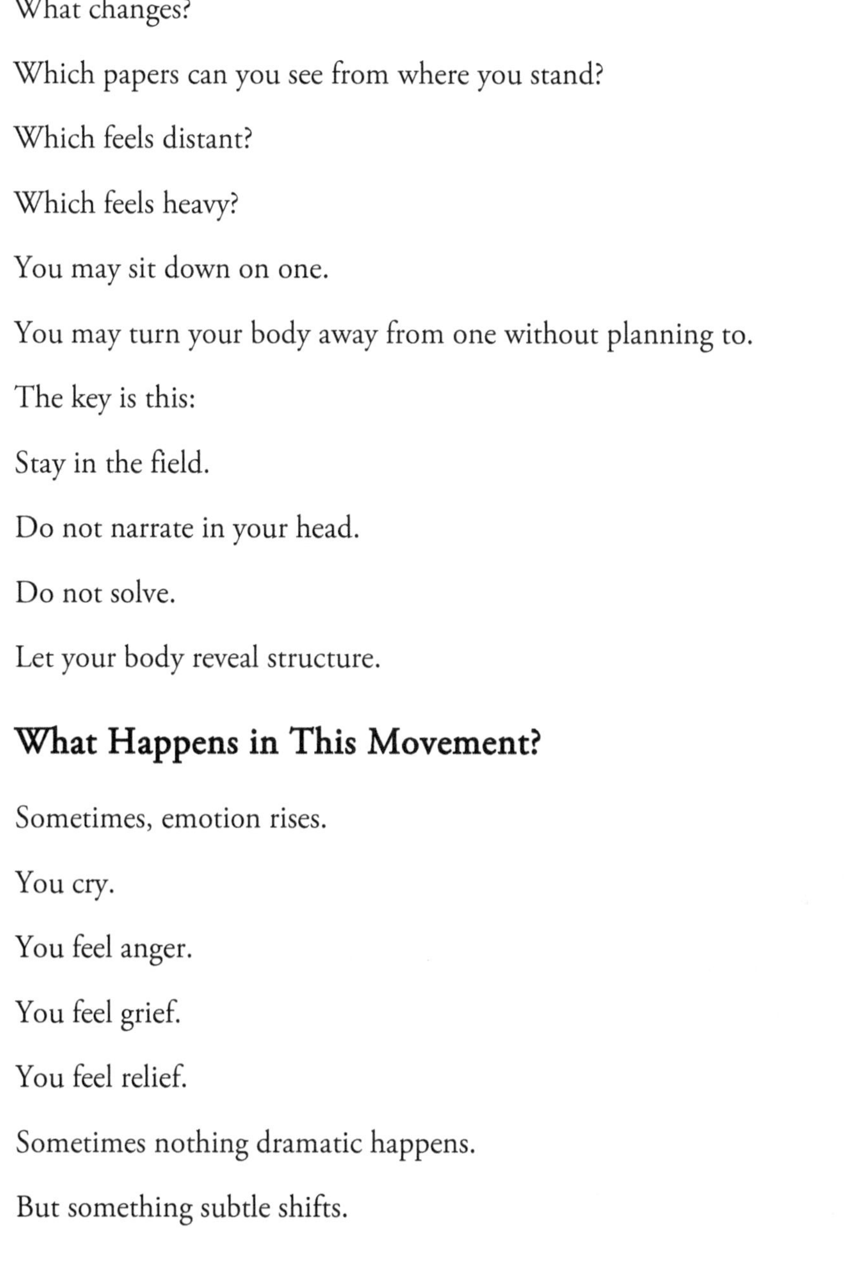

Stand again.

What changes?

Which papers can you see from where you stand?

Which feels distant?

Which feels heavy?

You may sit down on one.

You may turn your body away from one without planning to.

The key is this:

Stay in the field.

Do not narrate in your head.

Do not solve.

Let your body reveal structure.

What Happens in This Movement?

Sometimes, emotion rises.

You cry.

You feel anger.

You feel grief.

You feel relief.

Sometimes nothing dramatic happens.

But something subtle shifts.

In one ritual around my finances and work, I suddenly saw the direction clearly. The physical movement made it obvious which decision carried integrity and which did not.

In another ritual concerning my mother, I realized my entire body was turned toward her paper. Everything in my field revolved around that relationship. My work, my future, my children — they were barely in view.

That realization did not come from analysis.

It came from a position.

From field awareness.

Slowly, through repeated practice, I began to physically reposition myself in the ritual. I turned slightly toward my own path. Slightly toward my work. Slightly forward.

Over time, my real-life relationship with my mother shifted, too.

Not because I forced it.

But because my internal structure reorganized.

Step 4: Close the Ritual

When you feel complete — even if nothing dramatic happened — close the space intentionally.

Blow out the candle.

Gather the papers.

Say:

"This is enough for today."

Closure matters.

It prevents the field from remaining open and scattered.

What Processing Really Is

Processing is letting the story move.

It is allowing energy to settle.

It is letting experience find its rightful place in your internal architecture.

When something ruptures you — betrayal, loss, conflict — it creates disorganization in the field.

Ritual provides structure so that disorganization can reorganize.

Sometimes clarity comes immediately.

Sometimes integration is slow and subtle.

Both are valid.

Not Fixing — Integrating

This is important:

We do not enter ritual to fix other people.

We enter to integrate ourselves.

When you reposition in the field, your relational dynamics shift naturally.

You are no longer reacting to accumulated undigested material.

You are responding from a reorganized structure.

Bringing Ritual into Daily Life

Ritual does not need to be elaborate.

It can be:

- Five minutes at night reviewing your day.
- A candle lit before making a difficult decision.
- Writing one word on paper and standing with it.
- Sitting quietly and asking, "Where is my body turned?"

Ritual is repetition with intention.

And intention strengthens awareness.

Processing keeps your field clean.

It keeps your relations from hardening into unconscious structures.

It allows creation to remain fluid.

You live.

You take in.

You digest.

You reorganize.

You live again.

That is conscious living.

Not escaping life.

But allowing it to move through you fully.

Processing Through Relationship

Digestion is not always solitary.

Sometimes the field reorganizes best when it is spoken.

So let me ask you something simple:

Where do you process your day?

Not your trauma.

Not your biggest rupture.

Your day.

Let's say you were driving somewhere important and suddenly a giant cow blocked the road. Not for five minutes. For two hours. Everything shifted. Your schedule collapsed. You felt irritation, maybe fear, or maybe absurd laughter at the ridiculousness of it.

The whole day unfolded strangely after that.

Who do you tell?

Who do you process that moment with?

Because if you don't — it stays in you.

It may be small. But small undigested moments accumulate.

Processing can be as simple as coming home and saying:

"You won't believe what happened today…"

And in the telling — something moves.

The irritation softens.

The absurdity becomes humor.

The stress settles.

That is digestion.

Know Your Processing Space

It is powerful to know your processing space.

Ask yourself honestly:

Where do I let my day land?

For some, it is a journal.

For others, a walk alone.

For others, prayer.

For others, a partner.

For others, a voice note to themselves.

Processing through a partner can be beautiful — when it is mutual and safe.

This does not mean your partner must carry your emotional weight.

It means there is a space where you can speak freely, and in speaking, your field reorganizes.

And ideally, they also have a place to process — whether with you or elsewhere.

Processing must move both ways.

Otherwise, it becomes dumping.

Processing is an exchange.

The Difference Between Dumping and Digesting

Dumping is reactive.

Digesting is being aware.

Dumping sounds like:

"You always…"

"Everything is ruined…"

"I can't believe…"

Digesting sounds like:

"Today, something strange happened."

"I noticed I felt really tense."

"I'm still holding some irritation."

The difference is in tone.

In digestion, you are allowing movement.

In dumping, you are transferring charge.

Relational hygiene applies here, too.

You are not giving your undigested material to someone else.

You are letting it move through speech.

Speech itself is ritual.

It marks an experience.

It gives it shape.

It releases it from suspension.

Daily Micro-Processing

You do not need dramatic ritual every day.

Sometimes digestion is five minutes at the kitchen counter.

Sometimes it is sitting on the bed and recounting your day.

Sometimes it is writing three sentences in a notebook.

Sometimes it is silence — but intentional silence.

What matters is this:

Movement.

When experiences move, they integrate.

When they freeze, they accumulate.

Why This Matters

If you do not process the cow blocking the road, you may carry irritation into dinner.

If you do not process the awkward email, you may snap at your child.

If you do not process the subtle disappointment, it may quietly bond to resentment.

Processing prevents small moments from becoming structural tension.

It keeps your field fluid.

A Gentle Practice

Tonight, ask yourself:

Where did I process today?

Did I let anything move?

Or am I carrying it?

If you realize you are carrying something — small or large — find your space.

Speak it.

Write it.

Sit with it.

Ritualize it if needed.

Because digestion is not optional.

It is the maintenance of your inner architecture.

And when you digest well, your field stays clear enough to create again tomorrow.

PART FIVE

INFLUENCE - GUARDING YOUR FIELD

This chapter is direct on purpose.

Because this subject is not theoretical.

It shapes families.

It shapes health.

It shapes culture.

It shapes how people live — or how they live in fear.

If the field is your inner world — your creative, organizing layer — then the question naturally arises:

Can someone enter it?

Can someone steal from it?

Can someone tamper with it?

Across cultures, the answer has often been yes.

Devils.

Witches.

Demons.

Curses.

Destiny swapping.

Someone "taking your path."

Someone "stealing your luck."

These archetypes are ancient. They are powerful. And they are deeply embedded in many of our cultures — especially in South Africa, where accusations of witchcraft are not abstract ideas but lived realities.

So let us not dismiss them lightly.

Let us examine them carefully.

The Architecture Behind the Fear

If you believe someone can enter your field and steal your destiny before it manifests, what does that imply?

It implies that:

- Your field has no boundaries.
- Your creative system can be overridden.
- Your internal world is externally controlled.

That is a profound belief.

Because if that is true, then you are not the creator in your field.

And here is where we must be precise.

Influence is real.

Invasion is not.

Influence Is Real

We influence one another constantly.

Words influence.

Tone influences.

Culture influences.

Fear influences.

Stories influence.

If someone repeatedly tells you,

"Be careful. Someone is doing something to you,"

and you internalize it —

then you will create from that belief.

Your nervous system will tighten.

Your attention will scan for threats.

Your life may begin organizing around defense.

Not because someone hacked your field.

But because you created that structure once you internalized the idea.

Creation only happens through you.

Others may suggest.

Others may inspire.

Others may provoke.

But nothing is created inside your field without your participation.

A Personal Example

When I was younger, a close friend began telling people that I had stolen her path.

We had grown up together. I moved to study. She did not. Shortly after, mutual friends began calling me:

"She says you took what was meant for her."

At the time, I thought it was absurd.

But it showed me something important:

How powerful this narrative is.

The idea that destiny is transferable.

That someone else can take what was "meant" for you.

This belief does not arise from nowhere. It arises from cultural architecture — from archetypes that help people explain loss, disappointment, or inequality.

But explanation is not the same as truth.

When Belief Becomes Dangerous

I have seen families split over this.

In my own maternal family, my mother was accused of witchcraft.

The accusation began with a story: a cousin visited her house, later fainted, and claimed strange visions. A traditional healer was brought in. The story escalated. Suddenly, my mother was accused of trying to kill family members to gain wealth.

It was devastating.

Years later, the cousin admitted he had been high on drugs that day.

But by then, the damage was done.

The family never fully recovered. Relationships dissolved. Trust collapsed.

And the real issue — the boy's drug use — was ignored at the crucial moment when intervention could have helped him.

The archetype became the scapegoat.

"Someone did something."

That explanation became larger than the observable facts.

This is what happens when influence hardens into belief.

The Logic of Field Creation

Let us be clear.

If I sit in my room and perform a ritual wishing harm on someone, what am I working with?

Harm.

Resentment.

Destruction.

I am creating those qualities in my own field.

Field creation organizes first in the creator.

The idea that you can manipulate someone else's destiny without their participation is seductive — but it misunderstands how creation works.

You are the only creator in your field.

Others are stimuli.

You are the architect.

Ritual Is Not the Problem

Let's speak carefully about ritual.

Ritual is an ancient technology.

It is a focusing tool.

It helps you enter the field intentionally.

The problem is not ritual.

The problem is the belief that ingredients — bones, body parts, blood, objects — carry more creative power than consciousness.

I once spoke with a herbalist who described wealth rituals requiring animal parts — even human parts. He explained the symbolism: giraffe for height and victory, certain bones for strength.

Then I asked:

"What do you do after you gather these?"

He described days of isolation, reciting intention, staying focused, and anchoring desire.

And there it was.

The core was not the ingredient.

It was the focused intention.

The fear surrounding the ritual intensified belief — and belief, in turn, intensified creation.

But fear-based creation carries a shadow.

Because you are now organizing your life around guilt, secrecy, paranoia, and danger.

That is not wealth.

That is a distortion.

Influence vs. Entry

Let me make a simple analogy.

If someone steals money from your bank, they need access. They must hack security, physically enter, or obtain credentials.

Access is required.

The same is true in the field.

For someone to "enter" your field, they must be internalized by you.

You must accept the narrative.

You must believe the possibility.

You must give it space.

We may live in the same house.

We may share history.

But we do not inhabit the same field unless we align there.

Influence can knock.

But you open.

The Most Dangerous Intrusion

The most dangerous intrusion is not witchcraft.

It is suggestion.

If someone says to you:

"I sense something is wrong. Someone close to you is harming you."

Pause.

Do not reject instantly.

But do not internalize instantly either.

Process it outside of the suggestive field.

Speak to someone neutral.

Reflect privately.

Scan your own field calmly.

Because once that idea hardens inside you, it reorganizes your life.

You may become paranoid.

You may distrust those who love you.

You may scan constantly for betrayal.

That belief becomes self-fulfilling — not because someone hacked you, but because your field reorganized around the threat.

That is how influence works.

Field Hygiene

Just as you clean your house, you must clean your field.

Sweep out:

- Words that do not belong to you.
- Narratives that create fear without evidence.
- Suggestions that shrink your sovereignty.

Ask regularly:

What entered my field today?

What did someone say that lingered?

Is it true for me — or was it planted?

Not every thought you think originated with you.

But you decide what stays.

A Caution

In cultures where witchcraft accusations are common, fear becomes ambient.

People live scanning.

Scanning for envy.

Scanning for enemies.

Scanning for who might be stealing their luck.

That scanning itself is field distortion.

It creates fragmentation.

It creates illness.

Because the physical body organizes according to the conscious field.

Chronic fear in the field becomes chronic tension in the body.

Field hygiene is not spiritual vanity.

It is survival.

Sovereignty

You are influenceable.

Yes.

But you are not hackable.

No one can create in your field without your participation.

And if you find something inside you that does not serve you — fear, suspicion, resentment — you can process it out.

That is power.

Real power is not in attacking another's field.

Real power is maintaining clarity in your own.

Be careful what you let in.

Be careful what you rehearse.

Be careful what you harden into belief.

Because what you believe, you organize around.

And what you organize around — becomes your life.

The Layer Beneath the Narrative

When things in your life are not going well,

when relationships feel tense,

when money feels stuck,

when your body feels off,

when grief lingers longer than you expected —

the field feels disturbed.

And disturbance is uncomfortable.

The human system wants an explanation.

In cultures with strong witchcraft narratives, the explanation can arrive quickly:

"Someone has tampered with your field."

"There is bad luck."

"Someone envies you."

But if we pause — without dismissing the fear — we can ask:

What imbalance is actually present here?

Because there is almost always something real underneath.

Turbulence Is Not Always An Attack

Let us speak about context.

Many of us were born into turbulence.

I was born in Soweto. I loved it. I love it still. But it exists inside a larger historical rupture. Apartheid was not just political — it fractured families, opportunities, dignity, economics, trust. That rupture does not disappear in one generation.

Collective trauma becomes an ambient field.

Poverty creates stress.

Unemployment creates tension.

Unsafe environments create hypervigilance.

Historical injustice creates unresolved grief.

These currents move through people.

And when life feels unstable, it is tempting to personalize the turbulence.

"It must be someone."

But sometimes it is:

Grief not processed.

Stress not regulated.

Intergenerational fear not integrated.

Systemic imbalance playing out.

This does not mean nothing is wrong.

It means the wrongness may not be supernatural invasion.

It may be unprocessed turbulence.

Practical Field Scanning

When someone suggests to you,

"Something has been done to you,"

pause.

Instead of reacting, begin scanning.

Here are practical entry points:

1. Scan for Grief

Ask yourself:

What have I lost recently?

A person?

A version of myself?

An opportunity?

An expectation?

Grief unsettles the field.

If grief is unacknowledged, it can feel like bad luck or stagnation.

But it is simply an unfinished goodbye.

2. Scan for Chronic Stress

Is your body exhausted?

Are you sleeping well?

Is your nervous system constantly alert?

Are you carrying responsibilities alone?

Chronic stress distorts perception.

When your system is overloaded, ordinary challenges feel like curses.

Stress narrows vision.

Field awareness widens it again.

3. Scan for Relational Imbalance

Where is your energy turned?

Are you over-focused on one person?

Are you trying to fix someone?

Are you carrying guilt that is not yours?

Often, what feels like "tampering" is actually over-bonding.

Your field may be entangled — not invaded.

Entanglement can feel like a loss of power.

But it is different from attack.

4. Scan for Avoided Decisions

Is there something you know you must face?

A conversation delayed?

A career move postponed?

A boundary not set?

When we avoid decisions, the field becomes stagnant.

Stagnation feels heavy.

Heavy can be misinterpreted as cursed.

But stagnation is often postponed responsibility.

5. Scan for Internalized Narrative

Has someone recently said something that lingered?

"You are blocked."

"You are being attacked."

"You have bad luck."

Did you internalize it?

Because once you bond with that idea, your field begins to organize around it.

And you begin noticing only what confirms it.

This is how suggestion becomes manifestation.

Not through magic.

Through attention.

The Gap I See With Clients

When clients come to me convinced that they have been bewitched, I do not laugh. I do not dismiss.

I zoom out.

And from that distance, the imbalances become visible:

Unprocessed grief.

Financial fear.

Unhealed childhood patterns.

Chronic comparison.

Burnout.

Shame.

But inside the turbulence, they cannot see it.

So, the narrative of intrusion becomes relief.

It simplifies complexity.

"It's not me. It's someone else."

And in a way, that protects the ego.

But it also removes sovereignty.

Because once you believe someone else is the architect of your suffering, you stop scanning your own hinges.

The Hinges

I use the word hinge intentionally.

A hinge is a small mechanism that allows a door to move.

Tiny.

But crucial.

In the field, hinges are:

Beliefs.

Unspoken loyalties.

Hidden fears.

Avoided grief.

Chronic comparison.

When these are activated, the door of your life swings in a certain direction.

If you focus only on the door — "Why is this happening?" — you miss the hinge.

Field awareness trains you to look at hinges.

Responsibility Without Blame

This is delicate.

When we say,

"You are creating this,"

it must not mean,

"You are to blame."

Creation does not equal fault.

It means participation.

If grief is unprocessed, that is not your fault.

But it is your field.

If stress is overwhelming you, that is not shameful.

But it is affecting your perception.

If you internalize the idea of bad luck, that is understandable.

But once internalized, it organizes your life.

The power lies in noticing.

Reclaiming the Narrative

When someone says:

"Someone has done something to you,"

you can gently respond internally:

"Let me scan first."

And then:

Is there grief?

Is there exhaustion?

Is there stagnation?

Is there avoidance?

Is there inherited fear?

This does not deny that influence exists.

It places sovereignty back in your hands.

Because the moment you engage internally with the idea of being attacked,

you are giving that idea life.

And what is given life in the field — grows.

Cultivating a Language for Turbulence

Instead of:

"I am cursed."

We begin saying:

"My field feels unsettled."

Instead of:

"Someone stole my path."

We say:

"I feel behind, and I am grieving the version of life I imagined."

Instead of:

"I have bad luck."

We say:

"I am navigating systemic and personal turbulence, and I need to stabilize."

Language changes perception.

Perception changes organization.

Organization changes life.

This is the bridge.

Not dismissing culture.

Not mocking archetypes.

But helping people see that the very moment they bond to the idea of intrusion, they give it architecture.

Field awareness is not denial.

It is clarity.

And clarity restores authorship.

Conscious Living Is Presence

You have probably heard this before:

"Be present."

It sounds small. Overused. Almost cliché.

But presence is not a slogan.

It is the foundation of conscious living.

It is what stabilizes the field.

Bringing the Two Bodies Together

Once you understand the field, you understand something very practical:

You can be physically in one place

and consciously in another.

Your body may be on the floor playing a board game with your children.

But your conscious body is at work.

Or in tomorrow's deadline.

Or in yesterday's conflict.

So you are split.

Living in the present means bringing your two bodies into the same place.

If your physical body is here,

your awareness comes here too.

If you are with your children,

you enter the mother field fully.

If you are with a client,

you enter that field fully.

If you are with a friend,

you are nowhere else.

That is presence.

Why Presence Is Powerful

There is something I have noticed in my own life.

The reason I am good at what I do — especially in constellation work — is not because I am mystical.

It is because I am present.

When I enter a representation, I enter it fully.

When I leave, I leave fully.

Clients often tell me afterward,

"I don't know how you embodied that so exactly."

And often, I barely remember the details.

Because I was fully in that field —

and when it closed, I was fully out.

That is hygiene.

That is presence.

It prevents residue.

It prevents mixing fields.

A Teenage Practice

My relationship with presence started early.

The very first book I read was The Present by Spencer Johnson.

I must have been twelve or thirteen.

That book — and others like it — became a kind of teenage Bible for me.

Presence felt like power.

In a life where much felt unstable,

being present was something I could control.

And I practiced it.

Constantly.

Even without calling it field awareness, I was training it.

Why Presence Is Hard

Presence sounds easy.

Just be here.

But it requires order.

If your life is chaotic,

if responsibilities are unstructured,

if you have not handled what needs handling —

your field will be pulled constantly.

You cannot be fully present with your children

if you have unpaid bills you are avoiding.

You cannot be fully present with a friend

if your nervous system is unsure whether the babysitter must leave early.

Presence requires physical organization.

It requires that you take care of what you can.

Not perfectly.

But responsibly.

When Presence Breaks

There was a season when we moved countries.

New language.

New systems.

New schools.

New orientation.

Everything was unstable.

In that season, I could not stay present.

My body would be in one place —

but my awareness was scattered everywhere.

I was thinking ahead constantly:

Did I leave something undone?

What is the next appointment?

Did I understand that email in this new language correctly?

I was nowhere fully.

And I felt it.

I was doing so much —

but not grounded in any of it.

That was my cue.

It wasn't spiritual failure.

It was structural overload.

So, I slowed down.

I reorganized my physical life.

I created order.

I reduced noise.

I stabilized my nervous system.

And slowly, presence returned.

The Energy Difference

You can feel when someone is present with you.

You can also feel when they are not.

When I meet a friend, and I am truly there —

there is ease.

We laugh freely.

Time softens.

There is no urgency in the background.

When I am agitated internally —

counting babysitter hours in my head,

replaying emails,

thinking about dinner —

the energy changes.

I am physically there.

But I am not in the field.

And people feel that.

Children feel that.

Clients feel that.

Partners feel that.

Presence stabilizes the relationship.

Presence Is Field Hygiene

When you stay present:
You prevent field mixing.

You prevent residue.

You prevent chronic background anxiety.

You are not dragging yesterday into today.

You are not dragging work into your family life.

You are not dragging family into work.

You enter.

You participate.

You exit.

Cleanly.

Practical Cultivation

Presence does not happen by accident.

It is cultivated.

Small practices:

- When you sit down with someone, put your phone away fully.
- Before entering your home after work, pause for one breath. Leave the work field outside.
- Before opening your laptop, say internally, "Now I enter work."
- When you finish something, close it intentionally.

These are micro-rituals.

They align your two bodies.

Presence Is Sovereignty

Presence protects you from influence.

If you are here — fully here —

suggestions have less room to root.

If you are scattered,

fear slips in easily.

If you are grounded,

your field is stable.

Conscious living is not mystical elevation.

It is a grounded presence.

It is bringing your awareness home —

again and again.

And when your awareness and your body stand in the same place,

your life begins to feel whole.

Integration — Building a Regulated Life

Presence is the foundation.

But presence alone is not enough if your life is structurally chaotic.

Conscious living requires rhythm.

Rhythm regulates the field.

Children thrive on rhythm.

The body thrives on rhythm.

Even the earth moves in rhythm.

When your life has no rhythm, your field cannot settle.

What Is Regulation?

Regulation is not suppression.

It is not pretending you are calm.

Regulation means:

Your nervous system can return to baseline.

Your emotions can move without overwhelming you.

Your attention can focus where needed.

Your body feels mostly safe.

A regulated life is not drama-free.

It is recoverable.

You may be shaken.

But you return.

The Four Anchors of Stability

Let's make this practical.

If your field feels unstable, check these four anchors:

1. Sleep

Are you sleeping enough?
Not ideally — realistically.

Chronic sleep deprivation distorts perception. It increases paranoia, anxiety, and reactivity.

You cannot build a clear field on an exhausted nervous system.

2. Order

Is your physical environment manageable?

Not perfect.

But manageable.

Unfinished clutter creates background stress.

Unopened emails create background tension.

Unpaid responsibilities create background noise.

Order reduces invisible load.

3. Honest Conversation

Are you speaking what needs to be spoken?

Unspoken tension accumulates.

If you constantly suppress your truth, your field becomes congested.

Not explosive truth.

Responsible truth.

4. Meaningful Effort

Are you moving toward something?

A regulated life includes contribution.

When you feel stagnant for too long, the field turns inward and becomes heavy.

Even a small effort matters.

Learning something.

Building something.

Helping someone.

Forward movement is regulated.

When Life Is Structurally Overwhelming

Sometimes, instability is not personal failure.

It is the season.

New baby.

Migration.

Loss.

Illness.

Economic pressure.

In these seasons, your goal is not perfect presence.

It is minimal stability.

Reduce expectations.

Simplify commitments.

Lower the noise.

Conscious living includes compassion.

Integration in Daily Flow

Let me show you how this works together:

You wake up.

You scan lightly.

You handle what must be handled.

You enter work fully.

You exit work fully.

You process small irritations before bed.

You rest.

The next day begins lighter.

Over time, this builds something invisible but powerful:

Trust in yourself.

Trust that you can:

Notice.

Adjust.

Regulate.

Recover.

The Opposite of Fear

When people live in constant fear of being attacked, cursed, or tampered with, they live in hypervigilance.

Hypervigilance feels powerful.

But it is exhausting.

The opposite of that is not denial.

It is regulated sovereignty.

You do not scan for enemies.

You scan for alignment.

You do not obsess over intrusion.

You maintain hygiene.

You do not look outward for someone to blame.

You look inward for hinges to adjust.

That shift alone reduces anxiety dramatically.

A Quiet Test

Here is a small test for yourself:

When something goes wrong in your day,

what is your first internal sentence?

Is it:

"Who did this to me?"

Or is it:

"What needs attention here?"

That difference is the difference between reactive living and conscious living.

Living From Center

A stable field feels like this:

You are not easily pulled.

You are not easily convinced of catastrophe.

You are not easily thrown off by suggestion.

Not because life is smooth.

But because your center is anchored.

Presence.

Processing.

Regulation.

Rhythm.

This is not glamorous work.

It is daily work.

But it builds something rare:

A life that does not fracture easily.

And from there —

creation becomes cleaner.

Field Stability Is Not the Same as Wealth

Something has always fascinated me.

I have walked into homes in rural KZN where a hundred rand must last two weeks.

And there was rhythm.

There was laughter.

There was order.

There was a time when people gathered to eat.

There was cleaning time.

There was a system.

Very little furniture.

Very few resources.

But tranquility.

Then I have walked into homes — sometimes wealthier, sometimes not — where before you even reach the gate, you can feel something unsettled.

The same lack of resources.

But no rhythm.

No order.

No structure.

Only chaos.

And the field feels different.

That difference has nothing to do with money.

Poverty Does Not Automatically Equal Chaos

Yes, poverty can bring turbulence.

Stress.

Fear.

Scarcity thinking.

But poverty does not automatically create a chaotic field.

And wealth does not automatically create a regulated one.

A stable field comes from rhythm and order.

From clarity.

From structure.

From participation.

I Only Learned I Was "Poor" Later

I remember the first time someone described my childhood as "difficult."

I was in university. We were studying psychology.

My partner at the time said something like,

"You know, Promise comes from a very difficult background."

I felt like he was speaking about someone else.

Afterward, I asked him,

"What do you mean?"

He was shocked.

"What do you mean, what do I mean?"

Yes, we did not have much money.

Yes, my parents worked constantly.

Yes, I was alone with my sister for much of my teenage years.

But I loved my life.

I would not trade it.

I had freedom.

I had responsibility.

I had trust.

I managed money.

I ran a home.

I learned structure.

There was order.

My parents did not disappear randomly.

They called.

There were routines.

There were expectations.

There was communication.

It was unconventional.

But it was not chaotic.

That is the difference.

Structure Creates Stability

Field stability is not created by perfect family systems.

It is created by:

Clarity.

Rhythm.

Predictability.

Responsibility.

When I was a teenager, my father would leave money and instructions. I knew when to meet him at the taxi rank. I knew what my responsibilities were.

There was a system.

And system regulates.

Even with limited resources.

Even in unconventional structures.

The Difference Between Two Similar Circumstances

Why can two families have the same material circumstances — and yet one feels grounded and the other chaotic?

Because of the field organization.

One has:

- Defined roles
- Daily rhythm
- Clean physical space
- Clear expectations
- Emotional tone that is stable

The other has:

- Unspoken tension
- No rhythm
- No defined structure

- Chronic stress without processing
- Unclear boundaries

The difference is not income.

It is order.

Order Is Dignity

I have always admired elders who live with very little but maintain dignity.

An uncle of mine lives on very little. He sells on the street. He organizes his stock. He returns home. He makes it work.

He is peaceful.

He wakes up with direction.

That peace does not come from wealth.

It comes from alignment between:

Reality

Effort

Acceptance

Structure

He is not fighting his life constantly.

He is participating in it.

Chaos Is Not Poverty

Sometimes what we sense as "poverty" in a field is not a lack of money.

It is a lack of order.

There is a word we often use when we feel that energy before even entering a house.

You can feel it.

Not because there is no money.

But because there is no rhythm.

No regulation.

No system.

The field is scattered.

That is what destabilizes.

Your Primary Responsibility

This is why, in my life now, my number one focus is internal order.

Not perfection.

Order.

If my field is unsettled, no amount of money will calm it.

If my field is regulated, even turbulence can be navigated.

But internal order must be supported by physical order.

They are connected.

You cannot maintain presence if your life is structurally collapsing.

You cannot remain regulated if responsibilities are ignored.

So, we bring order externally where we can.

We pay what we can.

We communicate clearly.

We reduce chaos where possible.

We create rhythm.

Even a small rhythm regulates.

The Deeper Lesson

Outer wealth does not guarantee peace.

Outer poverty does not eliminate it.

Field stability comes from:

Clarity.

Participation.

Responsibility.

Rhythm.

Presence.

When you focus first on stabilizing your field — and then aligning your physical life as much as possible — you build something stronger than circumstance.

You build coherence.

And coherence is felt.

Before money.

Before status.

Before explanation.

It is felt.

And that is conscious living.

Comparison — The Silent Field Distorter

There is something that did not exist in the same way when I was growing up.

Constant exposure.

Constant visibility into other people's lives.

Today, you can wake up and within five minutes see:

Someone's new house.

Someone's new car.

Someone's vacation.

Someone's marriage celebration.

Someone's success announcement.

And even if you were peaceful five minutes before, something shifts.

Your field tightens.

You begin scanning.

"Am I behind?"

"Why not me?"

"What am I doing wrong?"

Comparison destabilizes rhythm.

Comparison Breaks Order

When you compare constantly, you step out of your own field.

You leave your rhythm.

You leave your timing.

You leave your resources.

And you enter someone else's structure.

Now you are measuring your life against a different context.

Different history.

Different opportunities.

Different system.

Different timing.

And the result is almost always dissatisfaction.

Even if your life was stable before.

The Illusion of "Being Behind"

One of the most common field disturbances I see is this:

"I feel behind."

Behind who?

Behind what timeline?

Behind whose expectation?

Comparison creates artificial urgency.

Artificial urgency creates stress.

Stress distorts perception.

Distorted perception looks like bad luck.

But often it is simply misalignment.

You left your field.

Returning to Your Rhythm

The question becomes:

What is my rhythm?

Not the global rhythm.

Not the Instagram rhythm.

Not the corporate rhythm.

Mine.

When I was young, my rhythm was different from my partner's childhood rhythm.

He had both parents home.

I had independence and responsibility.

Different structures.

Neither inherently superior.

Just different.

Peace came from accepting my rhythm — not comparing it.

A Practical Reset

If you feel unsettled, ask:

Have I left my rhythm?

Have I been consuming too much of someone else's life?

Have I forgotten what is actually working for me?

Sometimes the solution is not more effort.

It is less exposure.

Less noise.

Less comparison.

Return to:

What is required of me today?

What can I realistically manage?

What is already good here?

The Discipline of Enough

There is a discipline in saying:

This is enough for now.

Not as a resignation.

But as grounding.

Enough income for this season.

Enough progress for this month.

Enough growth for this year.

When you stabilize in "enough," your field softens.

You create from steadiness — not desperation.

And steady creation compounds.

Desperate creation fractures.

Living From Internal Measure

Conscious living means measuring your life from within.

Not from applause.

Not from status.

Not from visibility.

But from coherence.

Am I aligned?

Am I regulated?

Am I participating?

Am I present?

If the answer is mostly yes — you are not behind.

You are in your rhythm.

And rhythm builds quietly.

Over time, rhythm becomes strength.

And strength does not panic when others move faster.

It continues.

That is stability.

And stability is wealth.

Attention — The Currency of the Field

Where your attention goes,

structure follows.

This is not motivational language.

It is architecture.

If you give attention to fear daily, fear organizes your field.

If you give attention to possibility daily, possibility organizes your field.

If you give attention to resentment daily, resentment becomes structure.

Attention feeds.

And whatever you feed grows roots.

Stolen Attention

Earlier, we spoke about influence.

One of the most subtle forms of "theft" in the field is attention theft.

Not someone stealing your destiny.

Someone stealing your focus.

News cycles.

Social media outrage.

Family drama.

Endless comparison.

Constant crisis narratives.

These take your attention.

And once your attention is captured, your internal structure begins to reorganize around the object of attention.

You become reactive to what you repeatedly look at.

This is why some people feel chronically unstable without knowing why.

Their attention is scattered across twenty open loops.

No rhythm.

No containment.

No sovereignty over where their awareness rests.

Attention Is Direction

If attention is scattered, life feels scattered.

If attention is intentional, life feels directed.

When I was young and alone with my sister, there was one thing that protected my field:

Focused attention.

I was present with my responsibilities.

Present with my dreams.

Present with what was required.

I did not have endless distractions.

Today, distraction is everywhere.

Which means discipline must increase.

A Practical Audit

Try this for one week:

At the end of each day, ask:

Where did my attention live today?

Was it:

- In fear?
- In comparison?
- In problem-solving?
- In gratitude?
- In resentment?
- In a meaningful effort?
- In distraction?

Do not judge.

Just observe.

Patterns will appear quickly.

And those patterns reveal the architecture of your field.

Protecting Attention

Attention protection is not isolation.

It is filtration.

You do not need to consume every opinion.

You do not need to participate in every argument.

You do not need to respond to every suggestion.

When someone brings you a fear-based narrative, you can say internally:

"I do not feed this."

That is not denial.

That is discipline.

Deep Attention

There is also a positive side.

When you give sustained attention to:

- Your child's story.
- Your partner's words.
- A creative idea.
- A business plan.
- A moment of stillness.

Something deepens.

Attention builds intimacy.

Attention builds mastery.

Attention builds skill.

Scattered attention builds anxiety.

The Quiet Power of Focus

I have noticed something in my own work.

When I give my full attention to something — it moves.

Not because of magic.

Because energy consolidates.

A focused field has force.

A scattered field leaks force.

If you want stability, focus your attention on stabilizing practices:

Sleep.

Order.

Processing.

Presence.

Contribution.

Feed those.

Starve the noise.

Attention and Creation

Remember:

Creation happens through participation.

Participation requires attention.

If your attention is owned by fear, you create defensively.

If your attention is owned by comparison, you create anxiously.

If your attention is owned by purpose, you create steadily.

This is not abstract.

It is daily.

Every scroll.

Every conversation.

Every thought rehearsal.

One Final Question

Before you sleep tonight, ask:

What did I feed today?

Because what you feed today

will shape what you live tomorrow.

Attention is not small.

It is the steering wheel of your field.

Guard it.

Direct it.

And your life will begin to feel intentional rather than accidental.

That is conscious living.

Addictions — What the Field Is Trying to Solve

Addictions are not random.

They are solutions.

Not healthy ones.

Not sustainable ones.

But solutions.

When the field feels:

Overwhelmed.

Empty.

Unstable.

Lonely.

Hyper-alert.

Under-stimulated.

Something steps in.

Alcohol.

Sugar.

Scrolling.

Work.

Sex.

Control.

Shopping.

Drama.

Even spirituality.

Addiction always sustains something.

The question is:

What is it regulating?

The Systemic Role of Addiction

When I look at addiction systemically, I do not start with morality.

I start with a function.

What does this behavior provide?

Does it:

- Calm anxiety?
- Create stimulation?
- Provide belonging?

- Avoid grief?
- Replace intimacy?
- Offer identity?
- Offer escape?
- Offer structure?

For example:

A person who drinks every evening may not be addicted to alcohol.

They may be addicted to relief.

A person who scrolls for hours may not be addicted to the phone.

They may be addicted to distraction as a way of coping with inner turbulence.

Addiction stabilizes temporarily.

That is why it is powerful.

Addiction as Field Regulation

Remember:

If the field is chaotic, the body looks for relief.

Addiction becomes artificial regulation.

It narrows attention.

It changes chemistry.

It shifts perception.

For a moment, the field feels manageable.

That moment becomes reinforcing.

Repetition builds structure.

Structure becomes dependency.

When Addiction Becomes Identity

The danger is not the first use.

The danger is bonding.

When a person bonds identity to the regulating mechanism, the field reorganizes around it.

"I can't cope without this."

"I am like this."

"This is just how I relax."

That belief becomes architecture.

And architecture hardens.

Not All Addictions Look Dark

Some addictions are praised.

Work addiction.

Fitness obsession.

Spiritual superiority.

Productivity addiction.

These are socially rewarded.

But they can serve the same function:

Avoidance of deeper imbalance.

Addictions That Appear "Conscious"

We must also speak honestly about psychedelics and similar substances.

There is a growing narrative that certain substances help people "be present," "heal trauma," or "access the field."

And yes — altered states can temporarily widen perception.

They can loosen rigid structures.

They can dissolve defensive layers.

They can create powerful insight.

But here is the crucial question:

Are they supporting integration —

or replacing it?

If someone cannot access presence without a substance,

then presence has not been integrated.

The substance becomes the doorway.

And that can quietly become dependency.

The field must learn to stabilize without chemical assistance.

Otherwise, sovereignty is outsourced.

The Difference Between Tool and Addiction

A tool is used intentionally.

An addiction is used compulsively.

A tool supports long-term regulation.

An addiction bypasses it.

A tool strengthens your field.

An addiction replaces your field's self-regulation.

Even meditation can become an addiction.

Even healing work can become an addiction.

If it is used to avoid life instead of integrating life — it becomes an escape.

The Underlying Question

When you look at any behavior that repeats, ask gently:

What is this protecting me from feeling?

Not accusingly.

Curiously.

Is it:

Grief?

Loneliness?

Fear of failure?

Fear of success?

Shame?

Overwhelm?

Addiction is often an anesthetic.

Remove the anesthetic too quickly without addressing the wound — and the system panics.

So, we do not shame addiction.

We decode it.

Replacing Artificial Regulation

The solution is not willpower alone.

It is building alternative regulation:

- Sleep.
- Physical movement.
- Honest processing.
- Stable routines.
- Safe relationships.
- Meaningful effort.

When the field stabilizes naturally, the addictive behavior loses urgency.

Because it is no longer needed for survival.

A Gentle Reflection

Ask yourself:

Where do I reach automatically when I feel unsettled?

That reach tells you where your artificial regulation lives.

Then ask:

What would natural regulation look like here?

Not perfectly.

But slightly.

Small shifts reduce dependency.

The Deeper Compassion

Many addictions are born in turbulence.

In unstable childhoods.

In trauma.

In poverty.

In overstimulation.

In loneliness.

They are not signs of weakness.

They are signs that the field once had no other stabilizer available.

Conscious living does not judge addiction.

It restores choice.

When you understand the field, you understand this:

The goal is not to remove coping.

The goal is to build enough internal rhythm

that coping becomes optional.

And that is freedom.

Desire — The Movement of the Field

Desire is not the enemy.

Desire is movement.

Without desire, there is no creation.

No ambition.

No intimacy.

No learning.

No growth.

Desire is the field reaching forward.

But when desire is unconscious, it turns into craving.

And craving destabilizes.

The Difference Between Desire and Craving

Desire says:

"I would like to move toward this."

Craving says:

"I cannot be okay without this."

Desire expands the field.

Craving contracts it.

Desire can wait.

Craving demands.

When craving enters, rhythm disappears.

Urgency replaces presence.

How Desire Becomes Distorted

Desire becomes distorted when it attaches to identity.

"If I have this, I am worthy."

"If I achieve this, I am safe."

"If I get this person, I am complete."

Now desire is no longer movement.

It is survival.

And survival-driven desire creates turbulence.

Because nothing external can permanently stabilize identity.

Clean Desire

Clean desire is powerful.

It is:

"I want to build."

"I want to love."

"I want to create."

"I want to contribute."

Clean desire does not threaten your regulation.

It energizes it.

It aligns with rhythm.

You can move toward it steadily.

Without desperation.

Desire in a Regulated Field

When your field is stable:

You can want things without being consumed by them.

You can admire someone's success without feeling diminished.

You can pursue wealth without worshiping it.

You can desire partnership without abandoning yourself.

Regulation allows desire to remain creative.

Dysregulation turns desire into addiction.

The Cultural Layer

In environments shaped by scarcity — economic, emotional, or historical — desire often carries urgency.

"If I don't get this now, I may never get it."

That urgency is understandable.

But urgency must be examined.

Because chronic urgency exhausts the field.

It turns life into a constant chase.

Conscious living asks:

Is this desire aligned with my rhythm?

Or is it driven by fear of lack?

A Practical Reflection

The next time you want something strongly, pause.

Ask:

If I did not get this immediately, would I collapse?

If the answer is yes — you are not dealing with clean desire.

You are dealing with identity attachment.

And that deserves attention.

Not suppression.

But clarity.

Desire and Contentment

Contentment does not kill desire.

It stabilizes it.

You can be content — and still ambitious.

Contentment means:

"I am okay now."

From that place, desire becomes direction — not desperation.

You build steadily.

You pursue intentionally.

You rest without panic.

The Mature Relationship With Desire

Conscious living is not detachment from wanting.

It is maturity in wanting.

You do not suppress desire.

You regulate it.

You observe it.

You refine it.

You ask:

Is this coming from expansion?

Or from emptiness?

That question alone will transform many life decisions.

Desire is energy.

Addiction is misdirected energy.

Presence stabilizes energy.

And regulation channels energy.

When these are aligned,

your field becomes creative without becoming chaotic.

That is sustainable power.

And that is conscious living.

When Misfortune Looks Like Witchcraft

I just came out of a video call with three friends.

One of them has just gotten her first car. First license. First real independence on the road.

Within a short time, she knocked someone over — not fatally, thankfully — and shortly after that, she had another accident.

She is shaken.

And as she tells the story, the narrative forms:

"Someone close to me is bewitching me."

She says this confidently.

Because she went to a pastor.

And the pastor confirmed it.

So now the misfortunes are no longer random learning moments.

They are attacks.

She feels betrayed.

She feels targeted.

She feels vulnerable.

And you could feel it in her tone — she wanted validation. She wanted someone to say, "Yes. That must be it."

The Spiral Model

Then another friend speaks.

She tells a story about her grandmother in KZN.

Her grandmother has been "bewitched" for as long as she remembers.

Always sick.

Always under attack.

Always running from witches.

They moved villages multiple times trying to escape it.

Money was spent to make the house "strong."

And yet, the story continued.

Then she says something powerful:

"I wouldn't know if someone is bewitching me or not — because I'm not focused on that."

When something bad happens, she tells herself,

"Maybe something good is coming."

Same reality.

Different orientation.

What I Watched in That Moment

I said very little.

Because I could feel something delicate happening.

The first friend was tightening.

She did not want her narrative challenged.

She wanted it confirmed.

The second friend was gently trying to interrupt a spiral she has seen destroy a life.

Two orientations toward the same kind of turbulence:

One externalizes.

One reframes.

And this is the hinge.

Vulnerability and Narrative

When you are shaken — like after accidents, especially early driving experiences — you are vulnerable.

Your nervous system is already destabilized.

You are embarrassed.

You are afraid.

You are questioning yourself.

In that vulnerable state, suggestion enters easily.

If someone says:

"Be careful. Someone is doing something to you."

And especially if an authority figure confirms it —

the narrative roots quickly.

The field reorganizes around threat.

What could have been:

"I am learning to drive."

Becomes:

"I am under attack."

First Car Reality

When she was speaking, I gently said something neutral:

"First cars are a learning curve."

Because they are.

My first car? I had two accidents within a short period. One, because I trusted a parking attendant instead of checking myself. One, because I was inexperienced.

No witchcraft.

Just learning.

But when learning is framed as curse, growth turns into paranoia.

The Pattern Beneath

The deeper layer here is important.

This friend has a pattern.

When relationships end — someone bewitched her.

When things go wrong — someone is interfering.

There is a recurring external perpetrator.

And once that becomes a field habit, every turbulence confirms it.

Not because it is true.

But because the hinge is already installed.

The Most Dangerous Moment

The most dangerous moment is not the accident.

It is the interpretation.

Because interpretation shapes the field.

If you interpret turbulence as an attack,

your nervous system becomes defensive.

Defensive living creates more mistakes.

More mistakes confirm the attack.

And the cycle strengthens.

Why This Book Must Exist

What I witnessed on that call reminded me:

This narrative is deeply integrated.

It is not fringe.

It is not rare.

It is common.

And it is powerful.

Not because witches are powerful.

But because belief is powerful.

The moment you bond internally with the idea of being attacked,

you give it architecture.

Your attention organizes around it.

Your decisions shift.

Your relationships shift.

Your body tightens.

And your life slowly reorganizes around defense.

A New Reflex

Instead of:

"Who did this to me?"

We must cultivate:

"What is this teaching me?"

Instead of:

"Who is attacking my path?"

We must ask:

"Where am I inexperienced?

Where am I stretched?

Where am I learning?"

Not everything is growth.

But not everything is attack either.

Sometimes, a first car is simply a first car.

Sovereignty in Vulnerability

When you are vulnerable, protect your field carefully.

Do not accept the first explanation offered.

Especially explanations that remove your agency.

Pause.

Breathe.

Scan.

Is this fear speaking?

Is this embarrassment speaking?

Is this inexperience speaking?

Or is there truly evidence of harm?

Conscious living does not deny pain.

It denies automatic victimhood.

The Choice of Orientation

One friend lives scanning for witches.

One friend lives scanning for opportunity.

Same culture.

Same environment.

Different orientation.

And orientation determines field stability.

That call confirmed something for me.

The work is not just personal.

It is narrative.

We must reclaim authorship.

Because if we do not rewrite the interpretation,

we will continue living inside inherited fear.

And that is not conscious living.

That is repetition.

You are not powerless.

And most of the time — you are not under attack.

You are learning.

And learning feels unstable before it feels strong.

That is the difference.

And that difference must be understood.

Responsibility — The Return to Power

There is a subtle but powerful shift that happens when you stop asking:

"Who did this to me?"

And start asking:

"What is mine here?"

That question does not accuse.

It locates power.

When my friend has two accidents in a short period, the responsible question is not:

"Who is bewitching me?"

It is:

Am I distracted?

Am I anxious?

Am I rushing?

Am I overconfident?

Am I inexperienced?

Responsibility does not mean shame.

It means learning.

The Fear of Responsibility

Why is it easier to believe someone attacked you than to believe you are learning?

Because responsibility feels heavier.

If someone attacked you, you are a victim.

If you contributed, you must adjust.

Adjustment requires effort.

Victimhood requires vigilance.

Vigilance feels active.

Adjustment feels humbling.

Humility Is Stabilizing

Humility stabilizes the field.

When you say:

"I made a mistake."

The field relaxes.

Because now there is something you can improve.

When you say:

"Someone is doing something to me."

The field tightens.

Because now you must defend against invisible forces.

Humility creates growth.

Paranoia creates tension.

The Three Questions of Responsibility

When something goes wrong, ask three questions:

1. What was in my control?
2. What was outside my control?
3. What can I adjust next time?

This keeps your field balanced.

You do not over-blame yourself.

But you also do not over-externalize.

You stay centered.

Intergenerational Responsibility

This is especially important in cultures shaped by trauma.

We inherited:

Fear.

Hypervigilance.

Scarcity thinking.

Suspicion.

These were survival tools.

But survival tools do not always translate into peace.

We must consciously choose what we carry forward.

Responsibility means:

"I understand where this belief came from.

But I do not have to continue it."

That is how generational healing happens.

Not through ritual accusation.

Through an interpretation shift.

The Cost of Avoiding Responsibility

If my friend continues believing she is bewitched:

She will not refine her driving.

She will not slow down.

She will not practice more carefully.

She will scan for enemies instead of improving her skill.

And more accidents may follow.

Not because of witches.

Because of avoiding responsibility.

That is the quiet tragedy.

Responsibility and Self-Trust

Every time you take responsibility appropriately, you strengthen self-trust.

Self-trust stabilizes the field more than any ritual.

Because you begin to believe:

"I can navigate."

"I can adjust."

"I can learn."

That belief creates calm.

Conscious Responsibility

Conscious living is not about carrying everything alone.

It is about carrying what is yours.

You do not own:

Other people's projections.

Random events.

Systemic injustice.

But you do own:

Your interpretation.

Your response.

Your adjustment.

Your attention.

That is enough.

The Power Shift

The shift from:

"Something was done to me."

To:

"What can I refine?"

Is the shift from fear to authorship.

From chaos to order.

From reaction to creation.

And that is the heart of this entire book.

Because conscious living is not mystical protection.

It is mature participation.

You are not here to defend against invisible enemies.

You are here to learn, regulate, create, and adjust.

That is power.

Quiet, stable, undeniable power.

And once you taste that,

the narrative of attack loses its grip.

Helping Figures — The Architecture of Support

Earlier, we spoke about perpetrators in the field.

Now, let us speak about helpers.

I have always said that one of the greatest gifts humanity has ever received is the idea of God.

Not necessarily one specific religion.

But the idea that there is help.

That there is a larger intelligence.

That there is something that sees further than we do.

Across cultures, this idea takes different forms:

God.

Ancestors.

Angels.

Mother Mary.

Spirit guides.

Fairies.

Saints.

Protectors.

These are not random inventions.

They are helping architectures.

They are relational structures built into the field by generations of attention, prayer, devotion, longing, and hope.

And that matters.

Because whatever generations pour attention into becomes strong in the field.

First: Examine Your Relationship

Before using any helping figure, ask:

What is my relationship with this idea?

Is it fear-based?

Is it shame-based?

Is it transactional?

Is it comforting?

Is it regulating?

Is it oppressive?

For some, "God" feels loving.

For others, "God" feels judgmental.

For some, ancestors feel supportive.

For others, they feel demanding.

The figure itself is less important than the relationship.

Analyze honestly:

When I think of this helper, does my field expand or contract?

That tells you everything.

Helping Figures as Knowing Presence

Helping figures often represent something very specific:

The knowing presence.

The companion in uncertainty.

The witness who sees beyond your current confusion.

When I access my field through dreams, helpers appear.

Sometimes familiar.

Sometimes symbolic.

They offer clarity. Direction. A shift in perception.

But I do not leave it there.

I also sit consciously in the field — in meditation or stillness — and seek guidance.

And something remarkable happens consistently:

When I bring sincere attention to the knowing field, clarity arises.

Not always dramatically.

But steadily.

An insight.

A sentence.

A direction.

This is not superstition.

This is co-creation with awareness.

The field responds to focused attention.

Co-Creating With the Knowing Field

When you sit intentionally and say:

"I need guidance."

You are doing three things:

1. Slowing the surface mind.
2. Activating awareness.
3. Opening yourself to expanded perspective.

The "helper" may appear in the language you already know.

If you are a Christian, it may feel like Jesus speaking.

If you are ancestral, it may feel like your grandmother's spirit.

If you are secular, it may feel like intuition.

The language varies.

The mechanism is similar.

You are accessing the knowing layer of your field.

Honoring Your Language

I believe deeply in honoring the language you were given — if it still serves you.

If your grandmother lights a candle and calls the names of ancestors, and you kneel with her — be present.

In that moment, she is creating in her field with you in mind.

Her devotion is focused.

Her attention is anchored.

Her intention is clear.

That is powerful.

You do not need to reinterpret it.

You need to be present with it.

Because devotion is concentrated attention.

And concentrated attention shapes fields.

The Field Is Not Owned by One Tradition

The knowing field does not belong to one religion.

It is not confined to one doctrine.

It is not limited to one symbolic structure.

Over time, humans have built access points to it through different languages.

Some through prayer.

Some through ritual.

Some through meditation.

Some through song.

Some through silence.

The doorways differ.

The field of knowing remains accessible.

A Practical Way to Work With Helpers

If you have a helping figure you trust:

1. Sit quietly.
2. Name the issue clearly.
3. Address the figure directly in your own language.
4. Ask for clarity — not rescue.
5. Sit and listen.

Then watch what arises.

Not as hallucination.

But as orientation.

Often what comes is not external voice.

It is inner coherence.

The next right step becomes clear.

Beware of Outsourcing Responsibility

There is a balance.

Helpers support.

They do not replace responsibility.

If your helper tells you to drive carefully — you still must drive carefully.

If your helper encourages reconciliation — you still must speak.

If your helper offers courage — you still must act.

Helpers align you.

They do not live for you.

Mature Relationship With the Sacred

The most mature relationship with helping figures is not dependency.

It is partnership.

You bring:

Awareness.

Effort.

Responsibility.

You receive:

Clarity.

Strength.

Perspective.

That is co-creation.

The Gift of the God Idea

The God idea — in its healthiest form — reminds us:

You are not alone.

There is meaning beyond immediate turbulence.

There is intelligence beyond your current confusion.

That belief regulates the nervous system.

It creates hope.

Hope stabilizes the field.

And a stable field makes better decisions.

The Invitation

Instead of fearing intrusion, cultivate support.

Instead of scanning for enemies, build alliances.

Instead of asking:

"Who is against me?"

Ask:

"What wisdom is available to me?"

Because the field of knowing is always accessible.

And when you approach it consciously —

with clarity and responsibility —

it responds.

Not with magic.

But with alignment.

And alignment is help.

Imagination — The Bridge Between Worlds

There is something powerful about imagination.

Children use it freely.

Mystics use it consciously.

Artists live inside it.

Addicts sometimes escape into it.

Imagination is not fantasy.

It is a rehearsal space.

It is the bridge between the invisible and the visible.

Everything that exists physically was imagined first.

A house.

A business.

A book.

A system.

Someone held it internally before it became a matter.

Imagination is field architecture.

The Danger of Unconscious Imagination

If imagination is powerful, then we must be careful.

Because imagination does not distinguish between:

"I am cursed."

And:

"I am capable."

If you rehearse a curse internally long enough, your nervous system reacts as if it is real.

Your body tightens.

Your perception narrows.

Your decisions shift.

Imagination becomes lived experience.

That is why paranoia can feel real.

Because the field does not wait for proof.

It organizes around rehearsal.

Conscious Imagination

But imagination can also be used intentionally.

This is what I did unknowingly in my lucid dreams.

I rehearsed a life of calm, laughter, children near water, safety.

Years later, I stepped into moments that felt familiar.

Not because dreams are prophecy.

But because repeated internal orientation shapes external movement.

Conscious imagination is not a denial of reality.

It is an orientation toward possibility.

Helpers and Imagination

When you speak to ancestors, angels, God — what are you doing?

You are engaging imagination.

But imagination in this sense is not childish.

It is relational.

It activates:

Trust.

Hope.

Perspective.

It widens your internal field.

And from that widened space, wiser decisions often emerge.

The helper figure becomes a stabilizing anchor for imagination.

Fearful Imagination vs. Creative Imagination

There are two main directions imagination can go:

1. Defensive imagination
    o   What if something bad happens?
    o   What if someone harms me?
    o   What if I fail?
2. Creative imagination
    o   What if this works?
    o   What if I learn?
    o   What if I grow?

Both are powerful.

Only one builds stability.

Training the Imagination

We do not stop imagining.

We train it.

When fear-based imagination starts, pause and ask:

Is this protective or destructive?

If it is destructive, redirect gently.

Not by force.

By offering an alternative rehearsal.

"What if this accident is just a learning?"

"What if this setback is timing?"

"What if this turbulence is a transition?"

You are not lying to yourself.

You are widening the frame.

And widening the frame stabilizes the field.

The Creative Responsibility

Once you understand that imagination shapes perception, you cannot be careless with it.

You must ask:

What stories am I rehearsing daily?

Am I rehearsing an attack?

Or am I rehearsing growth?

Am I rehearsing scarcity?

Or am I rehearsing resourcefulness?

Am I rehearsing betrayal?

Or am I rehearsing trust?

Your imagination is not harmless.

It is formative.

Returning to Ground

The key is balance.

Imagination without grounding becomes delusion.

Grounding without imagination becomes stagnation.

Conscious living holds both.

You imagine a possibility.

You stay present in reality.

You seek guidance.

You take responsibility.

You rehearse strength.

You adjust behavior.

This is mature field work.

The Invitation Forward

You do not have to fear imagination.

You do not have to suppress helping figures.

You do not have to deny vulnerability.

But you must become conscious of how your inner narratives shape your field.

Because the field listens.

It organizes.

It responds.

And when you work with it intentionally,

you stop being carried by inherited stories.

You begin writing your own.

That is conscious living.

PART SIX
CONSCIOUSLY CREATING YOUR LIFE

Before we speak about money, status, or success — we must ask something deeper:

What does satisfaction feel like for you?

Not what does success look like.

What does your body feel like in a life that feels right?

Calm?

Engaged?

Useful?

Loved?

Creative?

Free?

Creation begins with internal clarity — not external comparison.

Step One: Define the Felt Experience

Many people say:

"I want a better life."

But better how?

More money?

More freedom?

More recognition?

More stability?

If you cannot define the internal experience, you cannot anchor it.

So, begin here:

If my life felt satisfying, what would my daily rhythm feel like?

Would I wake up peacefully?

Would I feel purposeful?

Would I feel unhurried?

Would I feel challenged in a healthy way?

The field responds to clarity.

Vague desire creates vague outcomes.

Clear orientation creates direction.

The Field Must See It First

Everything is created in the field before it becomes visible.

This is not mystical.

It is structural.

Before you change careers, you imagine it.

Before you build a home, you picture it.

Before you write a book, you hold it internally.

Creation begins as internal rehearsal.

This is where imagination becomes a tool.

Using Imagination Intentionally

Sit with the life you desire.

Not in fantasy.

In detail.

What does a normal Tuesday look like in that life?

Who are you around?

How do you move?

What responsibilities do you carry?

How do you speak?

Notice something important:

Often, the desired life is less about luxury

and more about regulation.

People want:

Stability.

Respect.

Time.

Meaning.

Harmony.

So instead of imagining a dramatic transformation, imagine small, sustainable changes.

Ritual as Anchor

Ritual is concentrated intention.

You do not need dramatic ingredients.

You need focus.

You can:

- Light a candle.
- Write your intention clearly on paper.
- Speak it aloud.
- Sit in silence and visualize.
- Close the ritual intentionally.

The power is not in the candle.

It is in the attention.

You are telling your field:

"This direction matters."

Repetition strengthens architecture.

Vision Boards and Contemporary Manifestation

Modern manifestation practices — vision boards, affirmations, scripting — operate on the same principle.

When you place images of your desired life before you, you are training your attention.

You are:

Priming perception.

Reinforcing possibility.

Strengthening orientation.

But here is the caution:

Visualization without alignment creates frustration.

You cannot visualize abundance and live in chronic chaos.

The field must be prepared.

Aligning Behavior With Desire

If you desire financial stability, ask:

Am I tracking my money?

Am I organizing my responsibilities?

Am I increasing my skill?

If you desire peaceful relationships, ask:

Am I regulating my reactions?

Am I communicating clearly?

Am I choosing wisely?

Desire without behavioral alignment becomes fantasy.

Desire with alignment becomes trajectory.

When You Feel Stuck

When people say:

"I feel stuck."

It usually means one of three things:

1. They are unclear about what they want.

2. They are afraid to move.

3. Their field is congested with unresolved past material.

First, clear congestion.

Process.

Stabilize.

Regulate.

Then clarify direction.

Then take small steps.

Not dramatic leaps.

Small, consistent shifts create momentum.

The Three Layers of Creation

To consciously create, you must work on three layers:

1. Internal Orientation

What do I believe is possible?

Do I feel worthy of this life?

2. Emotional Regulation

Can I tolerate discomfort while building?

Can I stay steady when progress is slow?

3. Practical Action

What skills must I develop?

What habits must change?

What relationships must shift?

Creation is not instant.

It is cumulative.

Satisfaction Is Personal

One person's satisfying life is rural rhythm and simplicity.

Another person's is urban expansion and ambition.

Neither is superior.

The key is alignment between:

Desire

Capacity

Values

Effort

When these align, satisfaction grows.

A Simple Creation Practice

Try this:

1. Write one sentence describing the life you want.
2. Write three qualities that life would require from you.
3. Begin practicing one of those qualities now.

If your desired life requires discipline — practice discipline now.

If it requires courage — practice courage now.

If it requires communication — practice communication now.

Become the person first.

Then the structure follows.

Creation Is Participation

The field does not reward passivity.

It responds to participation.

When you orient your imagination, anchor your intention, regulate your system, and take aligned action — your life begins shifting.

Not magically.

But systematically.

The Real Secret

The real secret of conscious creation is this:

You are always creating.

The only question is whether you are doing it consciously.

Every thought rehearsed.

Every fear repeated.

Every desire refined.

Every action taken.

It all builds structure.

So, choose carefully.

Because the life you desire

must first be stabilized internally.

Then rehearsed.

Then aligned with behavior.

Then repeated, until it becomes your new rhythm.

That is conscious creation.

And that is conscious living.

Time as Rhythm

Time has always fascinated me.

Not as something mechanical.

But as something living.

In my own work, I began to realize that we are not all moving on the same time.

We share calendars.

We share years.

We share deadlines.

But internally — we are orbiting differently.

When I look at our planet, I am always humbled.

The Earth has its own rhythm.

Its own speed.

Its own orbit.

And yet the planets next to it — they are also moving.

Different speeds.

Different distances.

Different timelines.

None of them is late.

None of them is early.

They are simply moving in their own rhythm.

That has always been such a profound lesson to me.

The way I orbit — is my own rhythm.

The Violence of Rushed Time

And yet today, especially with social media, we are living in rushed time.

Comparison time.

Announcement time.

Milestone time.

Everyone's engagement.

Everyone's promotion.

Everyone's pregnancy.

Everyone's expansion.

We are constantly exposed to other people's timelines.

And exposure creates pressure.

The Timeline Anxiety

I remember speaking to one of my sisters.

She was 26.

To me, 26 is young.

She said, "I'm not married. I don't have kids. This is the worst. I'm running out of time."

I remember feeling surprised.

Running out of time?

At 26?

I thought — this is such a beautiful season. To be free. To explore. To build. To know yourself.

But I could feel the pressure in her.

There was a timeline in her mind:

By this age — married.

By this age — children.

And if those milestones were not met, it felt like failure.

Not because she was unhappy.

Because she believed she was late.

Unspoken Timelines

There are timelines we inherit without realizing it.

Family timelines.

Cultural timelines.

Religious timelines.

Biological timelines.

Social timelines.

Some are spoken.

Some are silent but powerful.

And unless we consciously examine them, they begin to drive us.

Then we stop moving in our rhythm.

And start running in someone else's.

Creation and Impatience

I have noticed something interesting.

When it comes to grief — we allow time.

When someone dies, we understand that healing cannot be rushed.

When something tragic happens, we say, "Give it time."

We respect the slow unfolding of integration.

But when it comes to creation — we rush.

We plant today.

We expect the harvest tomorrow.

We start a business and expect stability next month.

We begin a relationship and expect permanence immediately.

We forget that creation also requires seasons.

Comparison — The Killer of Processing

Comparison interrupts rhythm.

It makes us distrust our own timing.

It tells us:

"You should be further."

"You should be faster."

"You should be there by now."

And once that thought enters, presence collapses.

Because we are not in our orbit now.

We are trying to jump to another.

But you cannot build depth in borrowed time.

You can only build it in lived time.

Allowing Time

Allowing time does not mean passivity.

It means a trusting process.

It means understanding that growth has stages.

Roots.

Stability.

Expansion.

Harvest.

If you try to harvest before the roots are strong, the structure collapses.

Time protects integrity.

Your Internal Clock

There is an internal movement inside you.

A quiet knowing of readiness.

Sometimes you are not ready — even if socially it seems you should be.

Sometimes you are ready — even if others think it is too soon.

Conscious living means listening to your internal clock more than the public clock.

That requires courage.

Because the public clock is loud.

The internal clock is subtle.

Time and Trust

When you trust time, anxiety softens.

You stop gripping outcomes.

You begin focusing on alignment instead.

You ask:

Am I building well?

Am I regulating?

Am I learning?

If yes — then timing will unfold.

Not perfectly.

But coherently.

The Invitation

When you feel rushed, pause and ask:

Is this urgency real?

Or is it comparison?

Is this deadline internal?

Or inherited?

Am I moving from alignment?

Or from fear of being late?

You are not behind.

You are in motion.

And motion, when aligned with rhythm,

is enough.

Time is not your enemy.

It is your ally.

If you allow it to be.

Trust — The Quiet Foundation

When rhythm is understood, trust becomes possible.

Trust is what allows you to move without panic.

Trust is what allows you to build without rushing.

Trust is what allows you to endure seasons without collapsing into fear.

Without trust, everything feels urgent.

With trust, everything feels workable.

What Is Trust in the Field?

Trust is the belief that:

- I can adjust.
- I can recover.
- I can learn.
- I can build.
- I can endure.

Trust is internal safety.

It is not the absence of problems.

It is the presence of resilience.

Distrust Creates Speed

When there is distrust, you rush.

You rush into relationships.

You rush into decisions.

You rush to conclusions.

Why?

Because somewhere inside, there is a belief:

"If I don't grab this now, I will lose."

Distrust accelerates time artificially.

Trust slows it down.

Building Trust Practically

Trust is not a personality trait.

It is built on evidence.

Every time you:

- Process instead of panic.
- Adjust instead of blame.
- Take responsibility instead of externalizing.
- Stay present instead of spiraling.

You strengthen trust.

Your nervous system begins to recognize:

"I survived that."

"I handled that."

"I can handle the next thing too."

That recognition stabilizes your field.

Trust and Creation

Creation without trust feels like gambling.

Creation with trust feels like building.

If you trust yourself, you can attempt things without collapsing.

If you do not trust yourself, every setback feels catastrophic.

Trust makes setbacks tolerable.

And tolerable setbacks make sustainable builders.

Trust and Helping Figures

This is also where helping figures become mature.

Not as rescue mechanisms.

But as reinforcement of trust.

When someone prays to ancestors or to God and feels supported, what often strengthens is not magic intervention — it is trust.

"I am guided."

"I am not alone."

"I am held."

That felt sense regulates.

And regulated people make clearer decisions.

When Trust Breaks

There are seasons where trust feels fragile.

After betrayal.

After failure.

After loss.

In those seasons, trust must be rebuilt gently.

Not through forced positivity.

Through small consistencies.

Wake up.

Do one thing well.

Keep one promise to yourself.

Rest when needed.

Trust grows through repetition.

Trust in Your Own Orbit

Return to the image of planets.

They do not question their orbit daily.

They move because the system holds.

Trust is like gravity.

Invisible.

But stabilizing.

When you cultivate trust, your life begins to feel less like an emergency and more like a movement.

The Three Levels of Trust

There are three levels:

1. Trust in yourself.
2. Trust in process.
3. Trust in life.

Trust in yourself means:

"I can respond."

Trust in process means:

"Growth takes time."

Trust in life means:

"Not everything is attack."

When these three strengthen, anxiety decreases dramatically.

The Calm Builder Revisited

The calm builder is not calm because life is easy.

They are calm because trust is strong.

They know:

Time is rhythm.

Setbacks are feedback.

Helpers are perspective.

Attention is currency.

Responsibility is power.

So they continue.

Not frantically.

But steadily.

Conscious living is not about controlling everything.

It is about cultivating enough trust

that you do not need to control everything.

And when trust anchors your field,

you stop reacting to every wave.

You begin navigating.

That is maturity.

And that is freedom.

PART SEVEN

EMBODIMENT - LIVING THE FIELD IN REAL TIME

Embodiment is not only about breathing deeply.

It is about living consciously inside what is happening.

It is bringing the field into daily life.

It is not retreating into philosophy.

It is not escaping into analysis.

It is staying with what arises.

Moving With the Current

Life does not wait for us to pause and meditate before it moves.

Arguments happen.

Children cry.

Deadlines collide.

Traffic frustrates.

Voices rise.

Very rarely do we stop mid-moment and say:

"Let me regulate."

Most of the time, the current sweeps us.

And that is human.

Embodiment does not mean never being swept.

It means being aware of what happened — during or after — and consciously processing it.

Naming What Is

For me, embodiment always begins with naming.

What actually happened?

Was that anger?

Was that fear?

Was that shame?

Was that protection?

In an argument, for example, you may spiral into anger.

If anger was needed — if a boundary was crossed — then anger is not wrong.

Anger is protective energy.

It says: "This matters."

But embodiment asks:

Was this anger clean?

Or was it layered with old material?

Did I defend appropriately?

Or did I over-defend?

Naming brings clarity.

Clarity prevents residue.

The Duck Story

I once heard a story told by Eckhart Tolle about two ducks in a pond.

They encounter each other and suddenly — fierce confrontation.

Flapping. Aggression. Territory.

Then they separate.

And within moments, both are peaceful again.

No grudge.

No story.

No replaying the fight in their heads.

The moment required defense.

They defended.

Then they returned to presence.

That is embodiment.

Clean Reaction vs. Residual Story

The problem is not reaction.

The problem is what we do afterward.

Humans rarely let the moment end.

We replay it.

We justify it.

We extend it.

We collect evidence.

Now the field holds the charge long after the situation has passed.

Embodiment means:

React when necessary.

Name what happened.

Process it.

Release it.

Return to the present field.

Being Present With What Arises

Embodiment is not about suppressing emotion.

It is about being present with it.

If sadness arises — feel it.

If anger arises — feel it consciously.

If joy arises — inhabit it fully.

Without dramatizing.

Without denying.

Without building an identity around it.

Just being in it.

Then moving on.

Pausing Is Ideal — But Not Always Realistic

Yes, ideally, we pause before reacting.

Yes, ideally, we calculate our response.

But daily life is dynamic.

Children do not wait for your mindfulness practice.

Conflict does not announce itself politely.

So, embodiment is less about perfect control

and more about conscious integration.

If you lost your temper — process it afterward.

If you overreacted — acknowledge it.

If you defended correctly — stand by it without guilt.

Processing prevents accumulation.

Field Awareness in Motion

Embodiment means knowing which field you are in.

If you are in a conflict field — stay there fully.

If you are in a creative field — stay there fully.

If you are in a nurturing field — stay there fully.

Do not drag the argument into dinner.

Do not drag work into play.

Move fields consciously.

That is maturity.

Presence Is Not Passivity

Being embodied does not mean being passive.

It does not mean being soft when firmness is needed.

It does not mean spiritualizing over injustice.

It means:

When firmness is required — be firm.

When softness is required — be soft.

When defense is required — defend.

When repair is required — repair.

And once the moment ends — let it end.

After the Wave

When you are swept by a moment, ask later:

What did that touch in me?

Was it only this situation?

Or something older?

This is where growth happens.

Not in preventing every reaction.

But in integrating what was revealed.

Embodiment is reflective participation.

Living Fully in Each Field

When you are with your children — be a mother fully.

When you are at work — be a professional fully.

When you are resting — rest fully.

When you are defending — defend consciously.

When the field shifts — shift with it.

That fluidity is embodiment.

Embodiment is not about controlling life.

It is about inhabiting it.

Fully.

Moment by moment.

Field by field.

And returning to presence after every wave.

That is conscious living in motion.

Not detached.

Not suppressed.

But alive.

PART EIGHT

REPAIR - THE ART OF RETURNING

No one lives consciously every moment.

No one regulates perfectly.

No one responds ideally every time.

You will:

Overreact.

Misunderstand.

Hurt someone.

Be hurt.

Speak too sharply.

Stay silent when you should have spoken.

The difference between unconscious living and conscious living is not mistake-free behavior.

It is repair.

Why Repair Is So Powerful

Repair restores rhythm.

When something ruptures and is not repaired, the field holds tension.

You can feel it in a home.

You can feel it in a marriage.

You can feel it in a friendship.

Silence becomes heavy.

Eye contact shifts.

Energy tightens.

Repair dissolves that accumulation.

The Ego Barrier

Repair is difficult because of the ego.

We want to be right.

We want to be justified.

We want to be understood first.

But conscious living asks something braver:

What matters more — being right, or restoring rhythm?

Repair Is Not Self-Blame

Repair does not mean taking responsibility for everything.

It means taking responsibility for your part.

"I reacted strongly."

"I spoke harshly."

"I misunderstood."

"I should have checked."

That sentence alone can soften an entire field.

Small Repairs Prevent Large Fractures

Unrepaired moments accumulate.

One small irritation.

Then another.

Then another.

Eventually, resentment becomes structure.

But small repairs — done quickly — prevent this.

A simple:

"I was overwhelmed earlier."

"I'm sorry for how that came out."

"Can we reset?"

Is field hygiene.

Repair With Yourself

Repair is not only relational.

It is internal.

If you broke a promise to yourself, repair it.

If you abandoned your routine, repair it.

If you lost presence for a week, repair it gently.

Self-attack does not build stability.

Gentle correction does.

Generational Repair

In cultures shaped by rupture, repair is revolutionary.

Where there has been silence, speak.

Where there has been an accusation, clarify.

Where there has been avoidance, engage.

Repair does not erase history.

It reorganizes its impact.

The Duck Revisited

The ducks fought.

Then they returned to peace.

Humans fight.

But we replay.

Repair allows us to return to the pond without carrying the fight into the next hour.

The Three Steps of Repair

1. Acknowledge what happened.
2. Take ownership of your part.
3. Restore connection.

No drama.

No performance.

No humiliation.

Just clarity.

Repair and Trust

Every successful repair strengthens trust.

Trust in yourself.

Trust in a relationship.

Trust in resilience.

Repair says:

"We are allowed to be imperfect.

But we are not allowed to stay disconnected."

Conscious Living Is Iterative

Life is not linear.

It is wave-like.

Rupture.

Repair.

Movement.

Adjustment.

Growth.

Embodiment allows rupture.

Repair restores flow.

Trust stabilizes.

Time integrates.

This is maturity.

Perfection is not the goal.

Continuity is.

When you know how to repair, you stop fearing conflict.

You stop fearing mistakes.

Because you trust your ability to return.

And that ability — to return consciously — is one of the strongest indicators of a regulated field.

That is conscious living in a relationship.

PART NINE
COMMUNITY AND COLLECTIVE FIELDS

When you walk into a room, you feel something.

Before anyone speaks.

That is a collective field.

When you return to a childhood home and immediately feel like you are "back in that role," that is a collective field.

When an entire community shares the same fear narrative — witchcraft, scarcity, suspicion — that is a collective field.

Collective fields are shared emotional atmospheres.

You Are Not Only You

This is important:

Sometimes what you think is "my anxiety,"

is actually a community field you are swimming in.

Sometimes what feels like "my fear,"

is inherited tension.

Sometimes what feels like "my limitation,"

is a cultural expectation.

When we spoke earlier about timelines and witchcraft narratives — those are collective fields.

They are not invented individually.

They are reinforced communally.

The Power of Collective Narratives

If an entire community believes:

"Success attracts attack."

Then, individuals who begin to succeed will feel tension.

Not because of actual sabotage.

But because they are moving against a collective narrative.

Collective fields regulate belonging.

When you step outside of a shared belief, you may feel:

Guilt.

Isolation.

Suspicion.

Pressure.

That is not magic.

That is social regulation.

Family Fields

Family fields are especially strong.

Roles are assigned early:

The responsible one.

The rebel.

The caretaker.

The failure.

The successful one.

And even when you grow beyond those roles, the family field may still see you through them.

Conscious living includes noticing:

Which parts of my identity are truly mine?

And which were formed inside a collective field?

Digital Collective Fields

Today, we also inhabit digital fields.

Social media is a collective emotional amplifier.

Fear spreads quickly.

Outrage spreads quickly.

Comparison spreads quickly.

If you consume too much of one emotional tone, your personal field begins to mirror it.

You must consciously regulate your participation.

Community as Stabilizer

Collective fields are not only destabilizing.

They can also regulate beautifully.

Think of:

A church gathering singing together.

A family meal where laughter is shared.

A community supporting someone in grief.

A group meditation.

Shared rhythm strengthens individual regulation.

Community can hold you when you are weak.

That is powerful.

Conscious Participation

The key question becomes:

Am I participating consciously in my collective fields?

Or am I being carried unconsciously?

You can love your culture

without absorbing every narrative.

You can honor your family

without inheriting every fear.

You can belong

without surrendering sovereignty.

Field Boundaries

You cannot control collective fields.

But you can manage your permeability.

Ask:

What narratives do I allow inside?

What conversations strengthen me?

What atmospheres destabilize me?

You are allowed to step back from collective fear.

You are allowed to choose a different orientation.

Changing a Collective Field

Here is something hopeful:

Collective fields shift when enough individuals shift.

When one person stops externalizing blame,

when one person takes responsibility,

when one person reframes misfortune as learning —

that ripple spreads.

You do not need to fight the entire culture.

You need to stabilize your own field first.

Stable individuals influence collective tone.

The Balance

Conscious living is not isolation.

It is grounded participation.

You belong.

You connect.

You contribute.

But you do not dissolve.

You stand in your rhythm

while engaging with others.

That is maturity inside a community.

Community and collective fields are real.

They shape us.

They influence us.

They regulate us.

But they do not define us completely.

When you become aware of the fields you inhabit,

you stop being unconsciously molded by them.

And you begin contributing to them intentionally.

That is conscious citizenship.

PART TEN
IDENTITY - THE STORY YOU LIVE INSIDE

Identity is not only your name.

It is not only your culture.

It is not only your profession.

It is not only your trauma.

It is not only your success.

Identity is the story your field repeats about who you are.

"I am strong."

"I am unlucky."

"I am the responsible one."

"I am the one who struggles."

"I am always attacked."

"I am always overlooked."

These sentences are architecture.

And architecture determines behavior.

Identity Is Rehearsed

You become what you repeatedly rehearse internally.

If you rehearse:

"I am behind."

You move anxiously.

If you rehearse:

"I am resilient."

You move steadily.

If you rehearse:

"I am cursed."

You scan for danger.

Identity is not static.

It is constructed through repetition.

The Invisible Contracts

Many identities are inherited.

You may have unconsciously agreed to be:

The stable one in the family.

The sacrificial one.

The successful one.

The one who never leaves.

The one who must prove themselves.

These identities are not chosen consciously.

They are absorbed through belonging.

But conscious living asks:

Does this identity still serve me?

Trauma-Based Identity

Sometimes identity forms around rupture.

"If I am vigilant, I am safe."

"If I am hyper-independent, I cannot be abandoned."

"If I expect betrayal, I won't be shocked."

These identities once protected you.

But protection strategies can become prisons.

You must ask gently:

Am I still living inside a survival identity?

Or am I ready for expansion?

Identity and Collective Fields

Remember what we spoke about earlier.

If your community holds certain narratives, identity often forms around them.

"If you succeed, people will attack you."

"If you are wealthy, you must have done something wrong."

"If you are unmarried by this age, you are failing."

If you internalize these, your identity shapes your ceiling.

Conscious living includes auditing inherited identity.

The Courage to Redefine

Redefining identity feels threatening.

Because identity is tied to belonging.

When you shift identity, others may feel uncomfortable.

If you stop being the "problematic one," the family must reorganize.

If you stop being the "rescuer," others must take responsibility.

If you stop being the "victim," you must take authorship.

That is uncomfortable.

But it is powerful.

Identity and Creation

You cannot create a life that contradicts your identity.

If you believe:

"I am not good with money."

You will unconsciously sabotage stability.

If you believe:

"I am not loved."

You will unconsciously test relationships.

If you believe:

"I am not capable."

You will hesitate when an opportunity arises.

Change identity, and behavior follows.

A Simple Identity Exercise

Write down the sentences that begin with:

"I am…"

Do not filter.

Then look at them.

Which ones are empowering?

Which ones are limiting?

Which ones are inherited?

Which ones are protective?

Then ask:

Which identity do I want to rehearse now?

Not dramatically.

But intentionally.

Becoming the Calm Builder

Earlier, we spoke about the calm builder.

That is an identity.

Someone who:

Trusts time.

Repairs quickly.

Embodies fully.

Regulates consistently.

Creates patiently.

If you begin identifying as that person, your decisions will align.

Identity shapes action.

Action reinforces identity.

That loop is powerful.

Identity as Choice

You are not required to remain who you were at 18.

You are not required to carry every narrative forward.

You are allowed to evolve.

Not recklessly.

But consciously.

Identity is not a betrayal of your past.

It is the integration of it.

When you become aware of your field,

aware of collective influence,

aware of rhythm,

aware of embodiment —

you realize something quietly radical:

You are not fixed.

You are forming.

And if you are forming,

you can choose what to strengthen.

Identity is not discovered once.

It is refined repeatedly.

And conscious living is the practice of refining who you are becoming.

I was scrolling and came across a live session.

A woman was celebrating her ex-husband's house burning down.

She showed the pictures repeatedly.

She was joyful. Almost triumphant.

She said she had waited twenty years for this.

She told her audience:

"If someone owes you money, just say it. Say may they suffer. Say may they be poor forever. That's what I did."

There were hundreds of people in the comments cheering.

Encouraging.

Validating.

And I found myself wondering:

What does this do to her field?

The Seduction of Vindication

There is something intoxicating about vindication.

When someone hurts you deeply —

and later something bad happens to them —

it can feel like balance.

Like cosmic justice.

Especially if you felt powerless at the time.

She was married at nineteen.

She says she was taken advantage of.

She waited.

She carried resentment.

So now, this moment feels like proof.

Proof that she was not crazy.

Proof that harm has consequences.

Proof that something heard her.

But here is the deeper question:

Does celebrating destruction regulate the field — or destabilize it?

Intention Is Still Intention

Earlier, we spoke about field creation.

We said: what you rehearse, strengthens.

What you feed, grows.

If you spend years saying:

"May they suffer."

"May they be poor."

"May something bad happen to them."

You are practicing destruction internally.

You are rehearsing harm.

You are shaping your nervous system around vengeance.

Even if the event that happened was a coincidence —

the emotional rehearsal was real.

And rehearsal shapes identity.

The Cost of Living in Revenge

Revenge feels powerful.

But it binds you to the past.

If your joy depends on someone else's downfall,

your field is still attached to them.

You are not free.

You are still in reaction.

Justice is different.

Justice restores order.

Revenge feeds destruction.

Justice vs. Revenge

Justice says:

"What happened was wrong.

I deserve protection.

I deserve restoration."

Revenge says:

"I want you to suffer as I suffered."

Justice builds systems.

Revenge builds fixation.

Justice releases.

Revenge loops.

The Field Does Not Freeze

The man's house burned.

He will rebuild.

He will adjust.

Life will move.

But if she frames those pictures —

if she anchors her identity around his destruction —

she freezes herself in that moment.

He moves forward.

She remains in the fire.

This is the tragedy of revenge.

It feels like victory.

But it prolongs attachment.

The Collective Celebration of Harm

What unsettled me most was not her joy.

It was the audience cheering.

Collective fields amplify vengeance.

When communities normalize wishing harm,

they reinforce scarcity consciousness.

"If you hurt me, I will destroy you."

"If I cannot have peace, you cannot have it either."

This keeps entire cultures in cycles of retaliation.

Not healing.

Does Wishing Harm Create Harm?

This is where field awareness becomes mature.

It is not about superstition.

It is about psychological architecture.

If you practice cursing, you strengthen anger.

If you practice bitterness, you strengthen resentment.

If you rehearse destruction, you normalize destruction.

The field you cultivate internally eventually reflects externally —

through tone, through choices, through relationships.

You may not burn someone's house.

But you may burn your own peace.

What Is Healthy Justice?

Healthy justice is structured.

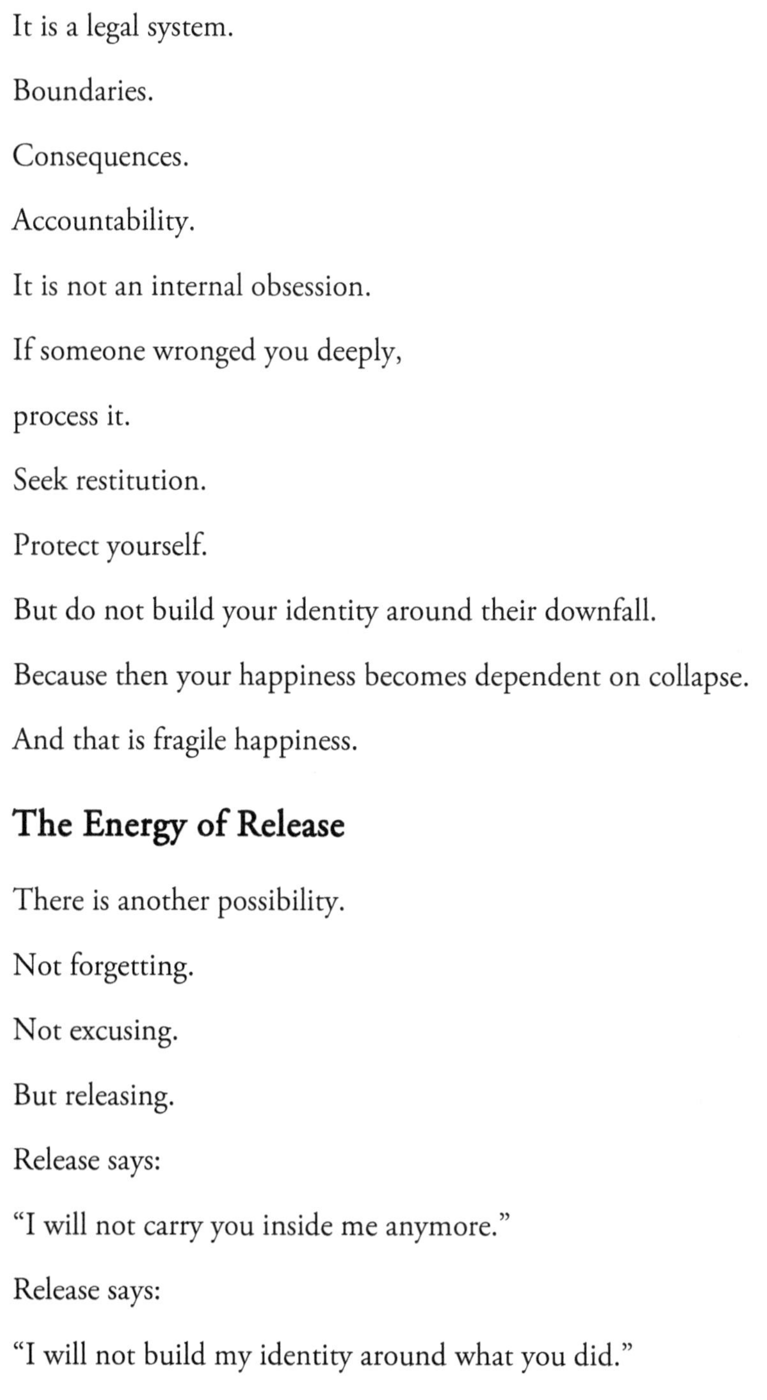

It is a legal system.

Boundaries.

Consequences.

Accountability.

It is not an internal obsession.

If someone wronged you deeply,

process it.

Seek restitution.

Protect yourself.

But do not build your identity around their downfall.

Because then your happiness becomes dependent on collapse.

And that is fragile happiness.

The Energy of Release

There is another possibility.

Not forgetting.

Not excusing.

But releasing.

Release says:

"I will not carry you inside me anymore."

Release says:

"I will not build my identity around what you did."

Release says:

"I choose my rhythm over your ruin."

That is strength.

Not cheering destruction.

But choosing sovereignty.

The Real Question

The real question is not:

Did she have the right to feel angry?

She probably did.

The real question is:

What future is she building by feeding this?

Because twenty years of rehearsal does not disappear.

It becomes personality.

It becomes tone.

It becomes orientation.

And orientation shapes destiny.

Conscious living does not deny anger.

It does not deny injustice.

But it asks something braver:

What do I want to become through this?

A person who celebrates destruction?

Or a person who restores their own life?

You cannot control what happens to others.

But you can control what you rehearse.

And what you rehearse,

you become.

That is the real field law.

PART TWELVE
THE ETHICS OF CREATION

Conscious creation is not neutral.

Every thought rehearsed,

every intention anchored,

every narrative repeated —

adds tone to the field.

You are not creating in isolation.

You are creating in a shared atmosphere.

When someone publicly celebrates destruction,

that energy does not disappear after the livestream ends.

It contributes to collective normalization.

And when hundreds cheer it on,

that reinforcement strengthens the pattern.

Creation is not just a personal manifestation.

It is participation in a moral atmosphere.

Intention Is Power

Earlier, we spoke about intention as anchoring.

Lighting a candle.

Speaking words.

Rehearsing desire.

But intention works in both directions.

You can anchor prosperity.

You can anchor healing.

You can anchor reconciliation.

You can also anchor harm.

The field does not filter for morality.

It responds to repetition and emotional charge.

This is why ethics matter.

Because power without ethics becomes destruction.

"They Deserved It"

The most dangerous phrase in revenge culture is:

"They deserved it."

Perhaps they did wrong you.

Perhaps they harmed you.

Perhaps they betrayed you.

But once you anchor yourself in their suffering as victory,

you align with destruction as nourishment.

And what nourishes you shapes you.

This is not spiritual superstition.

It is character formation.

Justice Without Corruption

There is a mature way to hold justice.

You can say:

"What happened to me was wrong."

"I deserve restitution."

"I will not allow this again."

And still not celebrate ruin.

Justice restores balance.

Revenge amplifies imbalance.

The difference is subtle but powerful.

Justice seeks order.

Revenge seeks satisfaction.

Order stabilizes the field.

Satisfaction fades and leaves residue.

What Are You Feeding?

When you engage with content that glorifies someone's downfall, ask yourself:

What part of me is being fed right now?

Resentment?

Vindication?

Bitterness?

Superiority?

Is this strengthening the person I want to become?

Or is it strengthening an older wound?

The ethics of creation begin with this question.

The Responsibility of Awareness

Once you understand field dynamics,

you cannot pretend your participation is neutral.

If you rehearse harm,

you increase tolerance for harm.

If you rehearse restoration,

you increase tolerance for growth.

You may not control outcomes.

But you control what you rehearse internally.

That is enormous power.

And an enormous responsibility.

Creation Beyond the Self

The deepest layer of conscious living is this:

You are not here only to manifest your desires.

You are here to refine the quality of your participation.

If your success comes through resentment,

your field remains unstable.

If your peace comes through someone else's ruin,

your peace is conditional.

Ethical creation asks:

Does my intention contribute to coherence?

Does my imagination build stability?

Does my reaction strengthen my character?

The Future You Are Becoming

Every repeated emotional rehearsal becomes personality.

Every personality becomes a pattern.

Every pattern becomes destiny.

Not mystically.

Psychologically.

If you rehearse bitterness for twenty years,

you become bitter.

If you rehearse restoration for twenty years,

you become restorative.

What are you practicing?

The Highest Form of Power

The highest form of power is not the ability to destroy.

It is the ability to refrain.

To say:

"I was hurt.

But I will not become harmful."

That is sovereignty.

That is maturity.

That is conscious living at its peak.

You cannot control what happens to others.

You cannot always control what happens to you.

But you can choose what you cultivate in response.

And that choice determines the atmosphere you carry.

And the atmosphere you carry

shapes the life you build.

That is the ethics of creation.

PART THIRTEEN
MEANING - THE COHERENCE OF A LIFE

Meaning is what makes suffering bearable.

It is what turns experience into wisdom.

It is what prevents chaos from feeling random.

Without meaning, life feels like a series of accidents.

With meaning, life feels like a movement.

Meaning Is Not Found — It Is Formed

Many people search for meaning as if it is hidden somewhere.

But meaning is formed through interpretation.

Two people can experience the same event.

One becomes bitter.

One becomes wiser.

The event is identical.

The meaning is different.

Meaning is the story you consciously build around experience.

Not Everything Is Positive

Meaning does not require that everything be good.

A betrayal can mean:

"I am unworthy."

Or it can mean:

"I learned discernment."

A loss can mean:

"Life is cruel."

Or it can mean:

"Love mattered deeply."

The difference is not denial.

It is framing.

Your Life as Narrative

When you zoom out on your life, you can see chapters.

Childhood.

Adolescence.

Early independence.

Transition.

Stability.

Reorientation.

Each chapter carries themes.

What themes are you living?

Are you living the chapter of reaction?

Or the chapter of integration?

Are you living the chapter of revenge?

Or the chapter of sovereignty?

You get to choose the tone of your narrative.

Meaning Stabilizes the Field

When something difficult happens, and you consciously form meaning, your field stabilizes.

Instead of asking:

"Why is this happening to me?"

You ask:

"What is this shaping in me?"

That shift prevents fragmentation.

It creates coherence.

Coherence reduces anxiety.

The Danger of Forced Meaning

Be careful.

Do not force meaning too quickly.

Grief must be felt before meaning emerges.

Anger must be acknowledged before wisdom forms.

Meaning that is rushed becomes spiritual bypassing.

Meaning that is digested becomes integration.

Living a Meaningful Life

A meaningful life is not necessarily dramatic.

It is aligned.

It feels like:

My actions match my values.

My rhythm matches my season.

My relationships match my boundaries.

My identity matches my growth.

Meaning is coherence between inner and outer life.

The Planet and the Orbit

Return to the image of planets.

Each one moves differently.

But none of them are random.

They are held in a relationship.

In gravity.

In rhythm.

Meaning is gravity.

It holds your experiences together.

Without it, everything feels scattered.

With it, everything feels connected.

When You Look Back

Imagine yourself years from now.

Looking back at this chapter of your life.

What meaning do you want to see?

That you were attacked?

Or that you were forming?

That you were unlucky?

Or that you were learning?

That you were reactive?

Or that you were becoming conscious?

You are writing that interpretation now.

Conscious Living

Conscious living is not control.

It is not perfection.

It is not avoidance of pain.

It is awareness.

It is participation.

It is a responsibility.

It is a regulation.

It is an ethical creation.

It is forgiveness.

It is meaning-making.

It is living your field with intention.

You began with questions about influence and intrusion.

You arrived at sovereignty and rhythm.

You moved through desire, addiction, attention, identity, community, embodiment, repair, ethics, forgiveness.

And now you stand here:

Not protected from life.

But capable within it.

That is conscious living.

And that is enough.

PART FOURTEEN
A HOLDING POINT

If you have come this far, something in you already knows:

This book was never about fear.

It was never about villains.

Never about perfect manifestation.

Never about controlling outcomes.

It was about reclaiming authorship.

You cannot control the weather of life.

You cannot prevent every rupture.

You cannot stop other people from acting from their wounds.

But you can regulate your participation.

You can scan your field.

You can clean your field.

You can choose what you rehearse.

You can choose what you build.

You can forgive.

You can slow down.

You can allow time.

You can form meaning.

You can return to presence.

Again and again.

The Practice Is Simple

Presence.

Processing.

Responsibility.

Rhythm.

Ethics.

Release.

Creation.

These are not complicated spiritual technologies.

They are daily movements.

And they will not always be elegant.

You will still react.

You will still get swept away.

You will still lose rhythm sometimes.

Conscious living is not about never falling out of alignment.

It is about noticing sooner.

Returning faster.

Repairing cleaner.

You Are Not Helpless

The narratives of intrusion,

of stolen destiny,

of hidden enemies,

of cursed paths—

lose power when awareness increases.

Not because the world becomes harmless.

But because you become grounded.

You understand:

Influence exists.

But authorship remains yours.

You understand:

Pain exists.

But identity is not confined to it.

You understand:

Time moves differently for everyone.

And your rhythm is not behind.

You understand:

Creation begins in imagination

but stabilizes in embodied action.

A Quiet Commitment

You do not need to declare anything loudly.

But you might quietly say to yourself:

I will participate consciously.

I will not build my life on resentment.

I will not rehearse harm.

I will not rush my rhythm.

I will not abandon presence.

I will live in awareness.

Not perfectly.

But intentionally.

This Is the Ground

Conscious living is not mystical.

It is deeply practical.

It is how you respond to a conflict.

How you sit with grief.

How you manage your time.

How you hold anger.

How you forgive.

How you create.

How you show up.

It is field work in ordinary life.

And that is sacred enough.

CLOSING

If you have walked with me through these pages, then you have walked through yourself.

We began with fear.

With influence.

With the question of intrusion.

With stories of witches, curses, misfortune.

We moved through rhythm.

Through presence.

Through addiction.

Through ethics.

Through forgiveness.

Through creation.

Through meaning.

Through embodiment.

And slowly, almost quietly,

the focus shifted.

From what is happening to me

to how am I participating?

That shift is everything.

Conscious living is not about becoming untouchable.

It is not about eliminating difficulty.

It is not about pretending the world is gentle.

It is about becoming internally anchored.

It is about regularly cleaning your field.

Processing what enters.

Releasing what no longer serves.

Creating with intention.

Allowing time.

Holding ethics.

Forgiving when needed.

Returning to presence.

Again.

And again.

You will still experience turbulence.

You will still lose rhythm sometimes.

You will still be triggered.

Hurt.

Overwhelmed.

But you will not be helpless.

Because you now understand:

Your field is yours.

Your participation is yours.

Your response is yours.

Your rhythm is yours.

Your creation is yours.

If there is one thing I hope you take with you, it is this:

Do not abandon yourself to narratives that shrink you.

Do not build your life around resentment.

Do not rush your timeline.

Do not outsource your authorship.

You are not here to fear life.

You are here to live it consciously.

And when you forget — because you will —

come back to something simple:

Where am I right now?

What is moving in me?

What needs digestion?

What needs release?

What needs intention?

Return to presence.

Return to awareness.

Return to yourself.

This is not the end.

It is simply a place to stand.

Grounded.

Aware.

Participating.

Consciously living.

And that is enough.